Monica's
KITCHEN

MONICA GALETTI

Monica's KITCHEN

Photographs by Yuki Sugiura

Quadrille
PUBLISHING

For David and Anais, my port in any storm

Publishing director **Jane O'Shea**
Creative director **Helen Lewis**
Project editor **Janet Illsley**
Art direction & design **Lucy Gowans**
Photographer **Yuki Sugiura**
Food for photography **Monica Galetti**
Props stylist **Cynthia Inions**
Production **Leonie Kellman, Vincent Smith**

First published in 2012 by
Quadrille Publishing Limited
Alhambra House, 27–31 Charing Cross Road,
London WC2H 0LS
www.quadrille.co.uk

Text © 2012 Monica Galetti
Photography © 2012 Yuki Sugiura
Design and layout © 2012 Quadrille Publishing Limited

Cataloguing in Publication Data: a catalogue record
for this book is available from the British Library.

ISBN 978 1 84949 103 7

Printed in China

NOTES

Use fresh herbs unless otherwise suggested.

Use organic or free-range eggs.

Buy unwaxed fruit if you are using the zest.

Timings in the recipes are for fan-assisted ovens.
If using a conventional (non-fan) oven, increase the
temperature by 15°C (1 Gas mark). Oven temperatures
can deviate significantly from the actual setting, so
use an oven thermometer to check the temperature.

CONTENTS

The one thing that unites the Roux family is without a doubt the pride and pleasure we get from seeing our protégés succeed. That we play a part in that success is a feeling on a par with giving pleasure to diners through our cooking.

Monica Faafiti, as she was called then, started her long and arduous road to stardom in the kitchens of Le Gavroche in 2000 as a young Kiwi chef with little experience of high-end cooking. By all accounts the first few months were tough, and many times I caught her grimacing and holding back the tears. But what I also saw in Monica was a drive and desire to do better, with an insatiable appetite to learn. Monica soon became a trusted Gavroche 'foot soldier', the type of battle-hardened cook that head chefs dream of. Never late, always there when you need them, no task too big or too menial. Give them a recipe, show them once and you know that it will always be followed to a tee. But soon after I saw another facet to Monica the 'work horse': creativity, now equally matched with all the necessary skills and knowledge to become a head chef. This coincided with my opening of Le Gavroche des Tropiques in Mauritius, a beautiful little restaurant that Monica gleefully took on as her own. Sadly it only lasted 18 months, but during that time the restaurant won many accolades due to the sumptuous menu and cooking skills of Monica.

Back in London, with more responsibility and input into the daily running of Le Gavroche, Monica has flourished even more. Her steely professional look is there for all to see and is testimony to the hard climb to the very pinnacle of her career. But look beyond that and you will see the most warm, affectionate, loving person and a beautiful doting mother. Monica is beyond doubt one of the finest chefs I have had the pleasure to work with and it fills me with joy to see her continue with her success. This book encapsulates the very essence that has made Monica an integral part of the Roux family.

I was born in Western Samoa, an island in the Pacific. My earliest memory

of food is of sitting in a cocoa tree sucking on the creamy sweet fruit that is dried to make chocolate, and my Aunty Pine telling me off, concerned that I might get an upset stomach. I was about 6 years old. To this day, dark chocolate is still my weakness, but the only person that tells me off for it is Michel, when I eat his stash in the kitchen office. I have worked for Michel for almost ten years now, and Le Gavroche is like a home for me. It's my playground. Since arriving on the doorstep back in January 2000, my gastronomic journey has taken a path that I could never have imagined, especially as a barefooted little girl running wild in the plantations in the Pacific Islands.

Working in such a revered kitchen has taught me so much about ingredients, the seasons and appreciating food – from its simplest of forms to the most intricate of recipes. From the beginning, Michel encouraged me to dine out and experience what other chefs are doing. I took his advice and have learnt so much from these amazing experiences. But eating well isn't all about restaurant food. To me, it is just as important to cook exciting, great-tasting food for my family and friends, and I bring everything I have learnt to my home kitchen.

In writing this book, I wanted to show you that it really is possible to serve fantastic food at home, if you use great ingredients and keep cooking techniques simple. It's just a case of thinking ahead a bit, so you have everything you need to hand. From Work to Table is the chapter that most reflects my current lifestyle, as I'm often looking to get a meal on the table straight after work. I hope it provides some quick and easy meals for you. Inevitably, time with my husband, David, and daughter, Anais, is limited, so we really try to make the most of it. At the weekend I enjoy cooking with Anais – baking cakes and making gnocchi and pasta, for example – while easy, slow-cooked casseroles and braises give us time to enjoy ourselves away from the kitchen. It is our Leisurely Weekend, relaxed and comfortable, that I'm sharing with you. Whenever the opportunity arises, I also love to indulge and entertain at home. The recipes in A Time for Friends are fun to prepare and a feast for the eye as well as the palate, so I hope you will find plenty of inspiration here when you are entertaining.

Finally, I wanted to bring you a taste of my Samoan background. Our style of food is based on family gatherings and the freshest of produce: vegetables grown on family plantations, meat from the family herds, fish fresh from the Pacific. There are also significant Chinese and South-east Asian influences. I have altered the traditional dishes to suit my style of cooking and modern tastes, so I hope I won't offend my forebears. Turn to Something Different when you fancy cooking something out of the norm, including my Samoan dishes.

From
Work
to Table

Roasted butternut squash soup
with crayfish tails

Serves 4

2 medium butternut squash
Olive oil for cooking
1 onion, peeled and thinly
   sliced
3 garlic cloves, peeled,
   halved and germ removed
2 tbsp pine nuts
1.5 litres vegetable or
   chicken stock (see
   page 184)
25g butter
250g cooked peeled crayfish
   tails or brown shrimps
Sea salt and freshly ground
   black pepper
2 tbsp single cream
   (optional), to finish

Heat the oven to 200°C/Gas 6. Peel, halve and deseed the butternut squash, then cut into chunks and place in a roasting tray. Drizzle with olive oil and season with a few pinches of sea salt. Roast in the oven for about 20 minutes until soft and caramelised.

Meanwhile, heat a drizzle of olive oil in a medium saucepan. Add the onion and sweat gently over a low heat for 7–8 minutes to soften. Add the garlic and sweat for another minute. Add the pine nuts and cook for a minute or two until lightly golden. Take the pan off the heat.

Once the squash is cooked, add it to the onion mixture. Return to the heat. Pour on enough stock to cover and bring to the boil. Lower the heat and simmer for 5 minutes.

Using a freestanding or handheld stick blender, blitz the soup until smooth, then pour back into the saucepan. Season with salt and pepper to taste and add enough of the remaining stock to give the required consistency. Heat through gently.

Melt the butter in a frying pan over a medium heat. Add the crayfish tails and gently warm through.

Spoon the crayfish into warm soup bowls and pour the butternut squash soup around. Finish with a drizzle of cream and serve with toasted wholemeal bread.

This is such a lovely comforting dish for a cold winter's evening. Pine nuts lend a wonderful flavour to the soup and crayfish tails and toasted rustic bread make it a filling supper.

Mediterranean puff tart

Serves 4

1 ready-rolled puff pastry
   sheet, about 35 x 25cm
10 cooked baby artichokes
   in oil, drained and
   quartered
10 sun dried tomatoes,
   halved
2 tsp small capers
1 large ball of mozzarella,
   about 150g
8 anchovy fillets in oil,
   drained
1 medium egg yolk, lightly
   beaten
Freshly ground black pepper
Handful of basil leaves,
   to finish

Heat the oven to 190°C/Gas 5. Lay the puff pastry sheet on a baking tray lined with baking parchment. Using the blunt edge of a knife, mark a 2cm border around the edge without cutting right through the pastry.

Scatter the artichoke wedges, sun-dried tomatoes and capers randomly over the pastry, leaving the border clear. Tear the mozzarella into pieces and distribute evenly over the tart. Tear each anchovy fillet in half or into thirds (as they can be quite strong) and sprinkle over the tart. Grind over some pepper.

Brush the pastry border with the beaten egg yolk. Bake in the oven for 15–17 minutes until the pastry rim is risen and golden brown and the base is crisp. Roughly tear the basil leaves and scatter over the tart. Serve hot, with a rocket salad.

I always have ready-rolled puff pastry in the freezer or fridge for convenient quick dishes. This one is great, not only as a midweek supper but also as a starter when you're entertaining. If I have some to hand, I brush the pastry with umami paste before applying the topping. For a special finishing touch, grind some basil leaves in a mortar with a pinch of sea salt and 2 tbsp olive oil and drizzle over the tart before serving.

Crayfish and celeriac gratin

Serves 4

160g celeriac
4 celery sticks
2 tbsp olive oil
4 medium eggs
400ml double cream
Freshly grated nutmeg
600g cooked peeled
    crayfish tails
Sea salt and freshly ground
    black pepper

Heat the oven to 180°C/Gas 4. Peel and coarsely grate the celeriac. De-string the celery, using a vegetable peeler, then slice thinly.

Heat a non-stick wide pan over a medium-low heat and add the olive oil. Add the grated celeriac with the celery and sweat for 2–3 minutes to soften without colouring. Take off the heat and set aside.

Lightly beat the eggs and cream together in a bowl, using a fork. Season with nutmeg and a little salt and pepper. Fold in the celeriac mixture and the crayfish tails.

Divide between 4 large ramekins or individual gratin dishes and bake in the oven for 12–15 minutes until bubbling and golden. Serve at once, with toasted baguette and a leafy side salad.

This is an excellent quick supper for the cooler winter months when celeriac is in season. We like to eat it with toasted baguette slices, lightly rubbed with garlic, and a side salad. The mixture can also be used as a quiche filling.

Pollock and saffron stew

Serves 4

700g skinless pollock fillet
Pinch of saffron strands
4 mild cooking chorizos,
  about 65g each
1 onion, peeled
2 carrots, peeled
2 celery sticks, de-stringed
  with a peeler
1 fennel bulb, trimmed
Olive oil for cooking
3 garlic cloves, peeled,
  halved, germ removed
  and sliced
1 tsp cumin seeds
1 tsp fennel seeds
2 tbsp plain flour
150ml white wine
500ml fish stock
  (see page 185)
Sea salt and freshly ground
  black pepper

Cut the pollock into 8 chunky pieces. Sprinkle with the saffron and a couple of pinches of salt and set aside. Remove the skin from the chorizos and slice or chop them.

Cut the onion, carrots, celery and fennel into bite-sized pieces. Heat a splash of olive oil in a large saucepan over a medium heat and add the vegetables with the garlic. Sweat for about 5 minutes to colour lightly.

Add the chorizo, cumin and fennel seeds and toss over the heat for a minute. Stir in the flour and cook, stirring, for a minute, then add the wine, followed by the fish stock, stirring.

Bring to the boil, then turn the heat down and season with salt and pepper. Simmer gently for 25 minutes, stirring occasionally. Place the pollock pieces on top of the stew, cover with the lid and cook gently for 3–5 minutes, depending on the thickness of the fish, until just cooked. Serve straight away.

This quick one-pot fish stew is ideal for an easy midweek family meal. Saffron may be an expensive spice, but you only need a pinch here to lend a subtle flavour and colour. If you can't get hold of the stamens, use powdered saffron instead, adding a bit more to achieve a good flavour.

Griddled tuna with cumin vegetables

Serves 4

4 tuna steaks, about
    140g each
Olive oil for oiling
Sea salt

Cumin vegetables
2 red peppers
2 courgettes
1 small aubergine
3–4 tbsp olive oil
2 tsp cumin seeds, crushed
2 tbsp sultanas
2 tbsp drained tinned
    chickpeas
Sea salt and freshly ground
    black pepper

Dressing
2 tsp wholegrain mustard
2 tsp mild curry powder
3 tbsp red wine vinegar
6 tbsp extra virgin olive oil

First make the dressing. Whisk the mustard, curry powder and wine vinegar together in a bowl, then whisk in the olive oil.

To prepare the vegetables, use a swivel vegetable peeler to remove the skin from the peppers, then slice off the tops and bottoms. Cut the peppers open, discard the core and seeds and cut the flesh into strips. Cut the courgettes and aubergine into thick batons.

Heat a large frying pan over a medium-high heat and add the olive oil. Now add the peppers, courgettes and aubergine and sauté for 4–5 minutes until lightly golden.

Sprinkle the crushed cumin and some salt and pepper over the vegetables and cook, stirring, for another 30 seconds or so. Take the pan off the heat and stir in the sultanas and chickpeas. Add 2 tbsp of the dressing and fold through, then check the seasoning; keep warm.

Heat a griddle pan until very hot. Season the tuna steaks with salt, rub all over with olive oil and place on the griddle pan. Sear for 1–1½ minutes, depending on the thickness of the steaks, until coloured and marked with the griddle, then turn and repeat on the other side for pink tuna.

Serve the tuna steaks immediately, with the warm cumin vegetables and the remaining dressing drizzled on top.

Tuna is a fish I prefer to eat either raw in a tartare or *mi-cuit* – just sealed on the outside and still very pink on the inside. Cumin is one of my favourite spices and it's particularly good matched with these Mediterranean vegetables, sweet sultanas and a light curry dressing.

Steamed salmon with soy and ginger

Serves 4

250g basmati rice
4 skinless salmon fillets,
   about 140g each
1 garlic clove, peeled and
   chopped
1cm piece fresh root ginger,
   peeled and grated
4 tbsp good-quality soy
   sauce
2 large handfuls of bean
   sprouts
Drizzle of sesame oil
3–4 spring onions, trimmed
   and sliced
Sea salt and freshly ground
   black pepper

To finish
2 tsp toasted sesame seeds
Handful of coriander leaves,
   roughly chopped

Tip the rice into a heavy-based saucepan or a rice cooker and add enough water to come at least 1.5cm above the level of the rice. Bring to the boil and cook until the rice is tender and dry, 10–12 minutes.

Meanwhile, check the salmon fillets for pin-bones, removing any you come across with kitchen tweezers. Place the salmon in a shallow dish, sprinkle with the garlic and ginger and rub well into the fish. Drizzle with the soy sauce and set aside to marinate for 5 minutes.

While the rice is cooking, bring the water in the steamer to the boil. Put the bean sprouts into the top of the steamer and drizzle with the sesame oil. Lay the salmon fillets on top, scatter over the spring onion slices and put the lid on. For lightly cooked pink salmon, which I prefer, steam for 1 minute only, then turn off the heat, lift the lid and position it so the steamer is partially covered. Set aside for a few minutes until ready to serve; the residual heat from the steamer will finish cooking the salmon to perfection.

(If you do not have a steamer, put the marinated salmon into a saucepan, add 100ml water and bring to the boil. Turn off the heat, add the salmon and cover with the lid. Leave to cook in the residual heat for 2 minutes. In the meantime, cook the bean sprouts in boiling salted water for a couple of minutes.)

To serve, place the salmon fillets on warm plates with the basmati rice and bean sprouts. Sprinkle the toasted sesame seeds over the rice and finish with a scattering of chopped coriander.

I came up with this recipe to please my daughter Anais, who loves a similar Thai dish she has at her best friend Alishar's house. I'm relieved to say that she wasn't disappointed.

Salmon with chorizo and peppers

SERVES 4

4 salmon fillets (with skin),
about 140g each
2 medium-hot cooking
chorizos
1 red pepper
1 yellow pepper
1 green pepper
2 shallots, peeled
2 tbsp pine nuts
Olive oil for cooking
12 cherry tomatoes
2 tbsp white wine vinegar
Sea salt and freshly ground
black pepper
Fine-quality balsamic
vinegar, to drizzle

Check the salmon fillets for pin-bones, removing any you come across with kitchen tweezers. Remove the skin from the chorizos and slice them, on a slight angle.

Use a swivel vegetable peeler to remove the skin from the peppers, then slice off the tops and bottoms. Cut the peppers open, discard the core and seeds and cut the flesh into strips. Slice the shallots into fine rings.

Heat a large frying pan over a medium heat, add the pine nuts and toast them quickly, tossing to colour all over, then remove and set aside.

Add 1 tbsp olive oil to the pan, then the peppers strips. Cook, turning, for 1 minute, then add the shallot rings and cook for another minute. Add the sliced chorizo and cook for 1–2 minutes. Add the cherry tomatoes and toss through lightly, then stir through the wine vinegar. Transfer to a warmed dish, add the toasted pine nuts and keep warm. Wipe out the pan.

Heat the frying pan again, over a medium-high heat, and add a drizzle of olive oil. Lightly season the salmon fillets with salt and pepper and place skin side down in the pan. Cook for 2 minutes, then turn the fillets over and remove the pan from the heat. Leave to stand for a minute; the salmon will finish cooking in the residual heat. I like my salmon pink in the middle, but you can leave it another minute or so if you prefer it a bit more cooked.

To serve, divide the chorizo and pepper mixture between warmed plates and place the salmon fillets on top. Trickle a little balsamic vinegar around the plates.

Salmon is a wonderfully versatile fish. Here, the addition of chorizo, peppers and pine nuts to pan-fried salmon fillets turns a standard evening meal into something much more interesting and enjoyable. Boiled new potatoes – tossed with butter, shredded parsley and seasoning – make an ideal accompaniment.

Trout on cucumber and broad bean ragoût

Serves 4

4 trout fillets (with skin),
  about 140g each
120g freshly podded
  broad beans
1 cucumber
4 tbsp olive oil
150g bacon lardons
700ml fish stock (see
  page 185) or vegetable
  stock (see page 184)
100g conchigliette pasta
Sea salt and freshly ground
  black pepper

Check the trout fillets for pin-bones, removing any you come across with kitchen tweezers. Using a sharp knife, lightly score the skin at intervals, on a slight angle.

Add the broad beans to a small pan of boiling water and blanch for about 3 minutes until tender. Refresh in cold water, then pop the bright green beans out of their tough outer skins into a bowl. Peel, halve and deseed the cucumber, then cut into batons.

Place a medium saucepan over a medium-high heat and drizzle in a little of the olive oil. Add the lardons and sauté until golden, then remove and drain on kitchen paper.

Pour the stock into the saucepan and bring to the boil. Add the pasta and cook for 5 minutes. Now add the broad beans and cucumber and cook for a further 2–3 minutes or until the pasta is cooked.

Meanwhile, heat a non-stick frying pan over a medium-high heat. Season the trout fillets on both sides with salt and pepper. Drizzle a little olive oil into the hot pan, then add the trout fillets, placing them skin side down. Cook for about 1 minute on each side, depending on thickness, until the fish is just cooked.

Once the pasta is cooked, the stock should have reduced down to a sauce consistency. Toss the sautéed lardons through the pasta and remove from the heat. Stir through the remaining olive oil and season with salt and pepper to taste.

Serve the trout fillets on the cucumber and broad bean ragoût.

I have used rainbow trout for this recipe but you can really use any fish you like, as the ragoût will complement white fish as well as other oily varieties, such as salmon trout and salmon. Again, you can substitute the broad beans and/or cucumber with whatever vegetables are in season.

Monkfish with lemon and caper butter

Serves 4

700g skinned, filleted
  monkfish tail
Olive oil for cooking
1 small Romanesco
  cauliflower, cut into
  small florets
Knob of butter
Sea salt and freshly ground
  black pepper

Cauliflower purée

1 medium cauliflower
50g butter
200ml double cream

Lemon and caper butter

1 lemon
1 tbsp olive oil
1 shallot, peeled and finely
  chopped
50g butter
Small bunch of parsley,
  leaves only, roughly
  chopped
1 tbsp small capers

Heat the oven to 180°C/Gas 4. For the lemon and caper butter, peel the lemon, removing all the white pith, then cut out the segments, free from the membranes. Cut into fine dice and set aside.

For the purée, chop the cauliflower into very small pieces and place in a large saucepan with the butter. Cook, stirring often, for about 6 minutes until the cauliflower is very soft and the butter turns a nutty brown colour. Pour in the cream, bring to a simmer, then take off the heat. Tip the mixture into a blender and blitz until smooth. Season with salt and pepper to taste. Set aside.

Season the monkfish fillets all over with salt and pepper. Heat a large ovenproof frying pan over a medium-high heat and add a drizzle of olive oil. Add the monkfish to the hot pan and colour for 2–3 minutes, turning as necessary, until golden brown on all sides. Transfer the pan to the oven for 2–3 minutes to finish cooking.

Meanwhile, add the Romanesco florets to a pan of boiling salted water and blanch for about 3 minutes until al dente. Drain and return to the pan. Toss with the knob of butter and season with salt and pepper. Gently reheat the cauliflower purée if necessary.

Transfer the cooked monkfish to a warm plate; keep warm. For the lemon and caper butter, heat the olive oil in the pan over a medium heat, add the shallot and cook for a few minutes until softened but not coloured. Add the butter and cook to a light nutty colour, then add the parsley, capers and lemon pieces. Remove from the heat. Taste and adjust the seasoning.

Spoon the cauliflower purée onto warm serving plates. Thickly slice the monkfish and place on top. Drizzle with the nutty butter and finish with the Romanesco florets.

Monkfish is one of my favourite fish to cook, as it has an excellent flavour, meaty texture and no fine bones at all! Romanesco, which is a cross between cauliflower and broccoli, is a lovely vegetable and it's now widely available.

Chicken goujons with paprika dressing

Serves 4

4 skinless chicken breast
  fillets, 500–600g in total,
1 medium egg, lightly
  beaten
100g polenta
Olive oil to drizzle
Sea salt and freshly ground
  black pepper

Paprika dressing

1 shallot or small onion,
  peeled and finely chopped
70ml white wine vinegar
2 tsp wholegrain mustard
2 medium egg yolks
1 tsp paprika
1 tsp mild Espelette pepper
  or dried chilli flakes, or
  to taste
200ml light olive or
  rapeseed oil

Heat the oven to 190°C/Gas 5. Slice each chicken breast on an angle into
3 or 4 long strips. Place in a bowl and season lightly with salt and pepper.
Add the egg and toss the chicken strips with a fork.

Lift the chicken strips out with the fork and place on a board. Sprinkle
with the polenta and turn the chicken to coat evenly all over.

Oil an oven tray. Lay the chicken strips on the tray and drizzle with a little
more olive oil. Cook in the oven for 7 minutes, turning halfway through.

Meanwhile, make the dressing. Put the shallot or onion and wine vinegar
into a small pan and bring to the boil. Let bubble to reduce by half, then
pour into a bowl and cool slightly. Whisk in the mustard, egg yolks and
spices, then slowly pour in the olive oil in a steady stream, whisking
constantly. Once the dressing has come together to a thick mayonnaise-
like consistency, adjust the seasoning with salt and pepper to taste.

When the chicken strips are ready, drain them on kitchen paper to
remove any oil, then serve straight away, with the paprika dressing.

This is a very quick recipe and so easy to make – even my husband
manages to knock it out for himself and our daughter when I'm working!
I like to make the paprika dressing quite spicy, but use less chilli if this isn't to
your taste. Serve with a simple rocket salad dressed with a little top-quality
balsamic vinegar and olive oil.

Poached chicken with soft polenta

Serves 4

4 large skinless, boneless
  chicken breasts, 180–200g
  each
16 basil leaves
4 slices of Parma ham
100g freshly podded broad
  beans
2 tomatoes
8 black olives, halved
  and pitted
4 tbsp olive oil
Squeeze of lemon juice
Sea salt and freshly ground
  black pepper

Soft polenta
800ml water
100g fine polenta
2 tbsp crème fraîche

First butterfly the chicken breasts. To do so, lay each chicken breast flat on a board and cut horizontally through the breast from one side almost to the other side, but keeping that edge intact. Open out like a book, so the breast is half the original thickness and twice the size.

Season the butterflied chicken breasts with pepper and a little salt (the Parma ham will add salt too). Lay a slice of Parma ham on each chicken breast and place 4 basil leaves on top. Now roll each chicken breast up to form a sausage shape and wrap in all-purpose cling film; tie each end with a knot to seal. Bring a large pan of salted water to a gentle simmer.

In the meantime, add the broad beans to a small pan of boiling water and blanch for about 3 minutes until tender. Remove with a slotted spoon, refresh in cold water, then pop the bright green beans out of their tough outer skins into a bowl.

Immerse the tomatoes in the boiling hot water for 30 seconds to loosen the skins, then refresh in cold water and peel. Quarter the tomatoes, remove the seeds, then cut into slivers and add to the broad beans.

Lower the wrapped chicken rolls into the pan of simmering salted water. Bring back to a simmer, then lower the heat and cook gently, turning now and then, for 7–8 minutes or until the chicken is just cooked through (open one to check).

Meanwhile, to cook the polenta, bring the water to the boil in a medium saucepan. Add the polenta in a steady stream, whisking as you do so. Cook, stirring, for 5–6 minutes until the polenta is thick and not at all grainy. Remove from the heat, stir in the crème fraîche and season with salt and pepper to taste.

Add the olives to the broad beans and tomatoes. Drizzle over the olive oil, add a squeeze of lemon juice to taste and season with salt and pepper. Remove the cling film from the chicken and slice each roll. Serve with the soft polenta and broad bean and tomato salad.

Wrapping each stuffed chicken breast in cling film holds it together and makes a perfect *ballotine*. Cooking the tightly wrapped parcels in barely simmering water seals in the flavours and guarantees moist, tender chicken. Once you have the knack of doing this, you can experiment with other fillings.

Glazed duck breast with pak choi and sweet potato mash

Serves 4

4 medium Gressingham duck
  breasts, 200–220g each
Olive oil for cooking
8 tbsp thin honey
6 tbsp soy sauce
4 pinches of ground ginger
Sea salt and freshly ground
  black pepper

Sweet potato mash
4 medium sweet potatoes
140ml milk, warmed
50g butter

Pak choi
4 pak choi, halved
  lengthways
25g butter
2 garlic cloves, peeled
  and crushed

Heat the oven to 190°C/Gas 5. For the mash, peel the sweet potatoes, cut into large chunks and place in a saucepan. Add water to cover and a good pinch of salt. Bring to the boil and simmer for 12–15 minutes until tender.

Meanwhile, trim any visible sinew from the duck breasts and score the skin with a sharp knife. Season all over with salt and pepper. Heat a large ovenproof frying pan over a high heat and add a drizzle of olive oil. Place the duck breasts skin side down in the hot pan and sear until golden brown, then turn and colour the flesh side briefly.

Transfer the pan to the oven and cook the duck breasts for a further 3 minutes, turning halfway through.

Add the honey, soy sauce and ginger to the duck in the frying pan and stir over a medium heat for about 20 seconds to reduce to a glaze. Spoon the glaze over the duck breasts and return to the oven for 1 minute. Set aside to rest in a warm place until ready to serve.

Drain the sweet potatoes once they are cooked and mash until smooth. Stir in the warm milk and butter and season with salt and pepper to taste.

To cook the pak choi, heat a little olive oil in a pan, then add the butter with the crushed garlic and allow to melt. Add the pak choi and cook for a minute or two until just wilted. Season with salt and pepper.

Halve the glazed duck breasts and place on warm plates with the pak choi, spooning over any remaining honey and soy glaze from the pan. Serve with the sweet potato mash.

I love duck, and what a treat it is to have it during the week.
This recipe is inspired by a wonderful chef friend of mine, Marcellin.
It is full of Asian flavours and includes pak choi – a fabulous vegetable
that goes particularly well with duck.

Seared steak with artichoke salad

Serves 4

4 rib-eye or sirloin steaks,
   about 180g each
Sea salt and freshly ground
   black pepper

Artichoke salad
2 large or 4 baby artichokes
1½ lemons
4 tbsp extra virgin olive oil
80g rocket leaves

To finish
20g Parmesan

First prepare the artichokes, one at a time. Pull off the outer leaves, then using a small paring knife, cut off the stem and cut away the thick outer skin to reach the heart. Use a teaspoon to carefully scrape out the hairy choke in the middle. Immediately immerse the artichoke heart in a small bowl of water with the lemon half added to prevent it discolouring. Repeat with the rest.

For the dressing, in a large bowl, whisk the juice of the remaining lemon with the extra virgin olive oil and season with salt and pepper to taste.

Heat a griddle or large frying pan over a high heat until very hot. Season the steaks with salt and pepper and add to the pan. Cook for 1 minute, then turn and cook on the other side for 1 minute. Remove to a warm plate and set aside to rest in a warm place for about 5 minutes while you prepare the salad.

Using a mandoline or swivel vegetable peeler, cut the prepared artichokes into very thin slices. Add to the dressing and toss well. Add the rocket leaves and toss through.

Slice the steaks and arrange on warmed plates. Top with the artichoke and rocket salad. Using a swivel vegetable peeler, shave the Parmesan over the salad to finish. Serve at once.

Fresh artichokes are so wonderful in salads, it's well worth mastering the technique of preparing them. The key to getting this dish right is to use a very hot pan to sear and colour the steak quickly, keeping the meat very pink and succulent – there's nothing more disappointing than chewy, overcooked steak.

Rump of lamb
with crushed cannellini beans

Put the lamb rumps on a board. Using a pestle and mortar, crush the allspice, rosemary leaves and 1 heaped tsp sea salt to a fine powder. Sprinkle the mixture evenly over the lamb and rub firmly to coat the rumps all over. Leave to marinate for 10 minutes.

Tip the cannellini beans into a saucepan. Add the garlic and stock and season well with salt and pepper. Bring to the boil, lower the heat and simmer gently until the stock has reduced by two-thirds. Remove from the heat and add the butter. Mash with a fork or blitz to a smooth purée in a blender (I like a fairly chunky texture so I use a fork). Keep warm.

Heat a large non-stick frying pan over a medium-high heat, then drizzle in 1 tbsp oil. Add the lamb rumps and cook for 2 minutes on each side until well coloured on the outside but still pink in the middle. Set aside to rest for 5 minutes before serving.

Spoon the crushed cannellini beans into a warmed bowl and sprinkle with a pinch of Espelette pepper. Put the yoghurt into a bowl and top with a sprinkling of lemon zest.

Serve the lamb rumps with the crushed beans, yoghurt and steamed or blanched tenderstem broccoli.

Serves 4

4 lamb rumps, about
   220g each
10 allspice berries
15 rosemary leaves
   (individual needles)
Olive oil for cooking
Sea salt and freshly ground
   black pepper

Cannellini beans
400g tin cannellini beans,
   drained
1 garlic clove, peeled,
   halved and germ removed
200ml chicken or vegetable
   stock (see page 184)
20g butter
Pinch of mild Espelette
   pepper flakes

To serve
200g Greek yoghurt
Finely grated zest of
   ½ lemon

These rosemary and allspice flavoured lamb rumps are quick and easy to marinate and cook for a special midweek meal. As the spice and herb rub keeps for a few weeks in an airtight jar, it's worth making up a bigger batch to have some to hand. The lemony yoghurt adds freshness and melts to form a no-fuss sauce.

Pork chops with Asian cabbage

Serves 4

4 pork chops, about
   210g each
Olive oil for rubbing
Sea salt and freshly ground
   black pepper

Asian cabbage
1 medium Hispi or
   Sweetheart cabbage
1 carrot, peeled
2 x 5cm pieces fresh root
   ginger, peeled
1 red chilli, halved and
   deseeded
2 tbsp olive oil
1 tbsp sesame oil
100ml soy sauce
Squeeze of lemon juice

Shred the cabbage, removing the core and any thick stems, and place in a large bowl. Thinly slice the carrot, ginger and chilli and cut into julienne strips. Add these to the cabbage and toss to mix.

Heat a griddle pan until very hot. Season the pork chops with salt and pepper and rub both sides with olive oil. Place the chops on the griddle pan and cook over a high heat for 3 minutes until well browned, then turn and repeat on the other side. Transfer to a warmed plate and set aside to rest in a warm place for about 5 minutes while you cook the cabbage.

Heat a large non-stick wok or sauté pan over a high heat, then add the olive and sesame oils. Tip the cabbage mixture into the wok and toss for a few minutes until starting to wilt. Add the soy sauce, toss through and remove from the heat. Add a squeeze of lemon juice, then taste and adjust the seasoning.

Serve the Asian cabbage immediately, with the griddled pork chops.

A quick cabbage, ginger and chilli assembly cooked in the wok peps up a simple pork chop. For me all that's needed to complete this meal is a bowl of steaming basmati rice.

Pork with prunes and Parma ham in pastry

Serves 4–6

2 pork fillets (tenderloins),
  about 400–450g each
20 ready-to-eat pitted
  prunes
2 sheets of ready-rolled
  puff pastry
10 slices of Parma ham
1 medium egg yolk, lightly
  beaten
Freshly ground white pepper

Heat the oven to 190°C/Gas 5. Trim the pork fillets of any sinew. Using a sharp knife, slice down the middle of each fillet without cutting all the way through, so you can open it out like a book. Season with pepper, then place 10 prunes in a line along the middle of each fillet. Bring the sides of the fillet back together to enclose the prunes.

Lay 5 slices of Parma ham on a board, overlapping them to form a sheet the same length as one of the pork fillets. Place the pork fillet on one end of the sheet and roll it tightly in the Parma ham.

Lay one of the puff pastry sheets on your work surface and place the Parma-wrapped pork fillet on one side. Wrap the puff pastry around the fillet, then trim off the excess pastry, leaving just a small overlap. Brush the edges with beaten egg yolk and press them together to seal. Repeat with the other pork fillet to make two parcels.

Brush the pastry all over with beaten egg yolk to glaze. Place the parcels on a large baking sheet lined with greaseproof paper and bake in the oven for 20–25 minutes until the pastry is crisp and golden brown. Leave to rest for 5 minutes before serving.

This is quick, simple and delicious. Wrapping the pork in Parma ham helps to keep it nice and moist. It also means you don't need to season the pork with salt. I like to serve this with a home-made apple compote and fried slices of black pudding.

Orzo pasta bake with smoked bacon and cheese

Serves 4

250g orzo pasta
1 tbsp olive oil
100g smoked bacon lardons
1 shallot, peeled and thinly
　sliced
6 button mushrooms,
　cleaned and quartered
100ml chicken stock
　(see page 184)
75g Comté cheese, grated
75g Gruyère cheese, grated
100ml double cream
Sea salt and freshly ground
　black pepper

Heat the oven to 180°C/Gas 4. Bring a pan of salted water to the boil. Add the pasta and cook until al dente, about 8 minutes.

Meanwhile, in a frying pan over a medium heat, heat the olive oil. Add the lardons and sauté for a minute until golden, then add the shallot and mushrooms and sauté for 2 minutes to soften.

As soon as the orzo is ready, drain it thoroughly and tip into a large bowl. Stir through the contents of the frying pan, the chicken stock, grated cheeses and finally the cream. Season lightly with salt and generously with pepper.

Pour the mixture into a baking dish and bake for 8–10 minutes until golden on the surface and bubbling. Let stand for 5 minutes before serving. A leafy salad is the perfect accompaniment.

Orzo is a fine pasta, shaped like grains of rice. It makes a great change from the more usual pasta varieties and works well in this creamy bake. Comté is a hard cheese from the Jura region of France, where my husband comes from. It is now widely available in good supermarkets. If you can get hold of one, I'd recommend using an aged Comté of around 18 months old.

Anais' pie with ham, spinach and egg

Serves 4

2 large handfuls of spinach
  leaves
Oil or butter for greasing
4 medium eggs, plus 1 extra
  egg yolk, lightly beaten,
  for brushing
200g sliced ham, roughly
  torn into shreds
200g cream cheese
1 sheet of ready-rolled
  puff pastry
Freshly cracked black pepper

Heat the oven to 180°C/Gas 4. Scatter a large handful of spinach leaves over the base of a lightly oiled or buttered baking dish, about 20 x 15cm. Break in 2 eggs, into opposite corners of the dish. Scatter half the ham evenly into the dish. Spoon half of the cream cheese on top, distributing it randomly, and season with some freshly cracked pepper.

Repeat these layers, breaking the eggs roughly into the other corners so they are distributed more or less evenly in the dish. Lay the sheet of ready-rolled pastry over the dish and trim away the excess pastry with a sharp knife. Dampen the rim of the dish and press the pastry edges firmly onto it.

Brush the pastry lid with the beaten egg yolk to glaze. At this stage, the pie lid can be scored with a pattern or shapes can be cut from the trimmings and stuck on with a little beaten egg. Bake the pie for about 20 minutes until the pastry is crisp and golden brown. Let the pie stand for 5 minutes before serving.

This is my daughter's favourite pie, most probably because she gets to make it from start to finish! It's a great recipe to get kids involved with, not least because they can have fun decorating the pie as they please. For contrast, I sometimes serve a lightly dressed leafy salad on the side, but you can have it on its own if you prefer.

Chicory salad with ox tongue and chestnuts

Serves 4

4 white chicory bulbs
4 red chicory bulbs (Treviso)
2 spring onions, trimmed
30 cooked peeled chestnuts
  (vacuum-packed)
8 large slices of ox tongue
  (from your delicatessen)

Dressing
4 tbsp crème fraîche
2 tbsp balsamic vinegar,
  or to taste
Sea salt and freshly ground
  black pepper

Trim the base off the chicory bulbs and discard the outer layer of leaves. Separate the rest of the leaves and place them in a large bowl. Finely slice the spring onions and add to the chicory with the chestnuts.

For the dressing, put the crème fraîche into a bowl and gradually whisk in the balsamic vinegar (the amount required will depend on the intensity of the vinegar, so taste as you go). Season with salt and pepper to taste.

When ready to serve, fold the dressing through the salad. Cut the tongue into broad strips and add to the salad. Serve immediately, with warm crusty bread.

This unusual salad is wonderful and you can enjoy it even if you don't like tongue – simply replace with sautéed bacon lardons or even leftover roast chicken. Or you can leave out the meat altogether and serve it as a colourful side salad.

Tartiflette of leeks and bacon

Serves 4

5 leeks, trimmed
4 slices of white bread,
  crusts removed
1 tbsp olive oil
60g smoked bacon lardons
25g butter
200g Reblochon cheese
200ml double cream
Sea salt
1–2 pinches of dried chilli
  flakes or freshly ground
  black pepper

Heat the oven to 180°C/Gas 4. Cut the leeks in half lengthways, wash thoroughly and slice thinly. Add the leek slices to a pan of boiling salted water and blanch for 1 minute, then drain thoroughly in a colander and set aside.

Cut the bread into 2cm cubes. Heat the olive oil in a large frying pan, add the lardons and sauté for a minute. Add the butter to the pan and allow it to melt and foam, then add the bread cubes and fry until golden. Drain the lardons and croûtons on kitchen paper.

Remove the rind from the cheese, then cut into small chunks. Tip the leeks into a large bowl and add the cheese, croûtons and lardons. Pour on the cream and toss to mix, then pour into an ovenproof dish.

Bake for about 10 minutes until the tartiflette is golden brown on top. Sprinkle some chilli flakes or pepper over the surface and serve.

Midweek, I love this all-in-one dinner. You can assemble it in minutes, then into the oven it goes and *voilà*! Dinner is served 10 minutes later. If you cannot get hold of Reblochon, use Raclette or Camembert instead.

Roast peaches with brioche croûtons and pistachios

Serves 4

4 ripe peaches
2 tbsp granulated sugar
25g butter
3 slices of brioche
2 tsp icing sugar
2 pinches of ground
  cinnamon

To serve
Vanilla ice cream
  (see page 187)
1 tbsp crushed skinned
  pistachio nuts

Heat the oven to 190°C/Gas 5. Cut the peaches in half and remove the stones.

Heat an ovenproof frying pan over a medium heat and add the sugar. Once it has melted and started to caramelise, increase the heat to high and place the peaches, cut side down, in the pan. Colour them lightly, then add the butter and stir to combine with the caramel and form a thick sauce.

Baste the peaches with the caramel sauce, then transfer the pan to the oven. Roast for 6 minutes, turning the peaches halfway through cooking; if they are quite firm, allow an extra minute or two on each side.

Meanwhile, cut the brioche into small cubes, dust with the icing sugar and scatter on a baking tray. Toast in the oven for 2–3 minutes. As you take the tray from the oven, dust the croûtons with the cinnamon.

To serve, divide the brioche croûtons between shallow serving bowls and place 2 roasted peach halves on each portion. Add a scoop of ice cream, sprinkle the crushed pistachios on top and serve at once.

This dessert is best made with very ripe peaches, so it's an ideal way to use up fruit that's just starting to over-ripen in the fruit bowl. If you decide to roast more peaches and have a few left over, keep them in a covered container in the fridge to serve the following day with plain yoghurt and any leftover brioche croûtons.

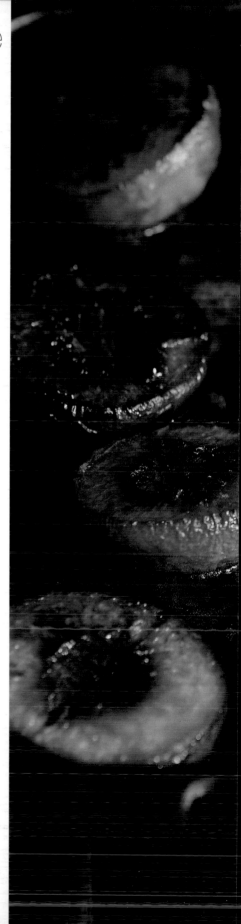

Griddled bananas with chocolate and cashews

Serves 4

4 ripe bananas
4 tsp rum
100g good-quality milk
  chocolate, chopped into
  small pieces
2 tbsp roughly chopped
  cashew nuts, toasted

To serve
Vanilla ice cream
  (see page 187)

Heat a griddle pan over a very high heat. Tear off 4 large squares of foil. Peel the bananas, halve lengthways and place a banana in the centre of each square of foil. Fold the edges of the foil up over the banana and twist together to form a sealed pouch.

Place the foil pouches on the griddle and cook for about 5 minutes, turning the pouches to cook the bananas on all sides.

Place a foil pouch on each serving plate, open up and carefully drizzle 1 tsp rum along each banana. Sprinkle the chocolate on top, then close the pouch again and leave to rest for 2 minutes; the chocolate will melt in the residual heat.

Open the pouches up again, sprinkle the toasted cashews on top of the bananas and serve at once, with a scoop of vanilla ice cream.

Friends tell me it's difficult to find time to make a pudding during the working week, but this is such a quick and easy sweet treat. More likely than not, you'll already have the few ingredients you need. I cook the bananas and add the chocolate just before the meal so it's melted and ready to enjoy warm after the main course.

Fruit compote with yoghurt, ginger and cinnamon

Serves 4

2 dessert apples
2 tbsp water
1 tsp sugar
2 bananas
20g butter
Squeeze of lemon juice,
  to taste
400g plain yoghurt
2 pinches of ground ginger
2 pinches of ground
  cinnamon

To serve
8 almond biscuits
  (see page 96)

Peel, quarter and core the apples, then cut into small chunks. Place in a small saucepan with the water and sugar and cook gently for 6–8 minutes until soft.

Meanwhile, peel the bananas and cut into chunks. Add to the apple with the butter and cook together for about 4 minutes until caramelised. Add a squeeze of lemon juice, then remove from the heat. Set aside to cool until warm, or completely as you prefer.

Divide the fruit compote between serving bowls and top each portion with yoghurt. Dust lightly with cinnamon and ginger. Serve with the almond biscuits – either whole or crushed and sprinkled on top.

This is a great way to use up odds and ends in the fruit bowl during the week. Or during the summer, if you have more berries than you need or some that are becoming too soft, mash them with a fork and use instead of the cooked fruit.

Lemon pain perdu

Serves 4

2 medium egg yolks
200ml double cream
60ml whole milk
2 tbsp caster sugar
2 tbsp olive oil
25g butter
4 slices of lemon cake,
   1.5–2cm thick (see
   page 99)

To serve
Vanilla ice cream
   (see page 187)

In a large bowl, beat the egg yolks, cream, milk and sugar together lightly with a fork until evenly combined.

Heat a large non-stick frying pan over a medium heat. Add the olive oil and butter and let it melt and foam.

Meanwhile, one at a time, dip the cake slices into the egg mixture to coat all over for 20–30 seconds (no longer or the cake will fall apart), then place in the hot pan. Fry for a couple of minutes until the underside is golden brown, then turn the cake slices over and repeat on the other side. They should be slightly crunchy on the outside, yet very soft in the middle.

Place a slice of pain perdu on each warm plate and top with a generous scoop of vanilla ice cream. Serve immediately.

This is one of my husband's favourites, probably because he can make it without having to bake the cake. In France pain perdu is typically made with sweet brioche, but it works brilliantly with this cake, as the zingy lemon marries well with the richness of the butter and egg batter.

A Leisurely
Weekend

Brioche with pink pralines

Serves 6

18g fresh yeast
40ml double cream
400g strong white bread
   flour
8g salt
70g caster sugar
1 vanilla pod, split and
   seeds scraped
4 medium eggs
240g butter, in pieces,
   softened
100g pink pralines, roughly
   chopped
1 egg yolk, beaten, to glaze

Mix the yeast and cream together in a small bowl.

In a large bowl, or the bowl of an electric mixer fitted with a dough hook, combine the flour, salt, sugar and vanilla seeds. Mix in the eggs, one at a time, then add the yeast liquid and mix until smooth. Now add the butter, a few pieces at a time, and mix until evenly combined and you have a very soft, smooth dough. Finally knead in the chopped pralines.

Place the praline brioche dough in a bowl dusted with a little flour. Cover the bowl with cling film and leave the dough to rise in a warm place for an hour or until it has doubled in volume.

Knead the dough lightly, then shape into a ball and place on a baking sheet or form into an oblong and place in a 500g loaf tin. Leave in a warm place to prove until doubled in size, about 30 minutes. Meanwhile, heat the oven to 200°C/Gas 6.

Brush the brioche with beaten egg yolk. Bake for 10 minutes, then lower the oven setting to 180°C/Gas 4 and bake for a further 20 minutes.

NOTE Pink pralines are almonds with a pretty pink sugar coating. You can buy them in good delicatessens and specialist confectionery shops; they are also available online.

This version of brioche, speckled with crushed pink pralines and vanilla seeds, is lovely for breakfast or brunch, or as a treat at any time of the day with coffee or tea. You can make the dough, shape it and leave it to rest in the fridge overnight, ready to prove and bake first thing in the morning. It never lasts long in our house, but if there is any left over, I'll make pain perdu or a bread and butter pudding.

Creamed onion soup

**Serves 4 as a light lunch,
or 6 as a starter**

5 white onions, peeled
1 medium potato
2 tbsp olive oil
1 garlic clove, peeled, halved
  and germ removed
150g piece of smoked
  bacon, derinded
500ml chicken stock
  (see page 184)
300ml double cream
Sea salt and freshly ground
  black pepper
4 tbsp crème fraîche,
  to serve

Croûtons
2 thick slices of white bread,
  crusts removed
Olive oil for cooking

First make the croûtons. Cut the bread into small cubes. Either toss them in a little olive oil and place on a baking tray in the oven preheated to 180°C/Gas 4 for 8–10 minutes, or fry them in a little oil in a hot non-stick frying pan, turning to colour all over, for 2–3 minutes until crisp and golden; keep warm.

For the soup, thinly slice the onions and cut the potato into chunks. Heat the olive oil in a frying pan over a medium-low heat. Add the onions and sweat gently for about 5 minutes to soften without colouring.

Add the potato to the onions with the garlic and bacon. Continue to sweat gently for another 10 minutes. Season with a little salt and a generous grinding of pepper. Now pour in the chicken stock and bring to the boil, then lower the heat and simmer gently for about 20 minutes.

Lift out the bacon and set aside; keep warm. Add the cream to the soup and bring back to the boil, then take off the heat. Transfer the soup to a blender and blitz until smooth. Taste and adjust the seasoning.

Cut the bacon into pieces. Divide the soup between warm bowls and top each portion with a spoonful of crème fraîche. Scatter over the bacon pieces and croûtons and serve.

This is a wonderful soup – both filling and delicious – for those chilly winter days or evenings when you need something warming and comforting. If you can get new season's onions, you'll find that their sweeter, more delicate flavour makes a real difference to this soup. You can serve it as a starter, or with plenty of warm bread and perhaps some cheese as a lunch or supper.

Scrambled eggs *with crab*

Serves 4

8 medium eggs
320g fresh white crabmeat
25g salted butter
1 tbsp chopped chives
Sea salt and freshly ground
  black pepper
4 thick slices of country loaf,
  toasted, to serve

Crack the eggs into a bowl and beat lightly with a fork. Pick over the crabmeat, discarding any fragments of shell.

Heat a heavy-based non-stick saucepan over a very low heat. Add half of the butter and allow it to melt, then pour the egg mixture into the pan, stirring with a wooden spoon.

Continue to stir the eggs until they start to clump together. Add the crabmeat and the remaining butter. Gently fold through the scrambled eggs and remove from the heat.

Season with salt and pepper to taste and sprinkle with the chopped chives. Pile onto hot toasted country bread and serve immediately.

This is a great way to start the weekend – either for breakfast or brunch. Using fresh white crabmeat is a must for me, but if you can't get hold of the fresh shellfish, you can opt for smoked salmon instead.

Walnut and pear salad with a creamy Roquefort sauce

**Serves 2 as a lunch,
or 4 as a starter**

Caramelised pears

3 firm, ripe Conference pears

1 tbsp granulated sugar

25g salted butter

100ml sherry vinegar, plus
   a little extra for the
   dressing if needed

Salad

1 white chicory bulb,
   trimmed

1 red chicory bulb (Treviso),
   trimmed

1 Gem lettuce

30g rocket leaves

2 tbsp chopped chives

1 tsp walnut oil

1 tbsp olive oil

100g walnut halves

Sea salt and freshly ground
   black pepper

Roquefort sauce

150ml double cream

100g Roquefort, cut into
   pieces

Heat the oven to 180°C/Gas 4. For the sauce, put the cream and Roquefort in a saucepan and heat gently until the cheese has partially melted (there should still be some small chunks; don't let it boil. Remove from the heat and set aside.

Peel, halve and core the pears, then cut into thick wedges. Scatter the sugar in a non-stick ovenproof pan and heat gently until melted, then cook to a light golden caramel. Add the pear wedges and toss to coat in the caramel. Add the butter and allow to melt, then stir the sherry vinegar into the buttery caramel. Spoon the caramel sauce over the pears until they are well coated and golden, then transfer the pan to the oven and cook until the pears are soft, about 5 minutes.

Meanwhile, for the salad, separate the chicory and lettuce into leaves and toss them with the rocket and chives in a large bowl. When the pears are ready, transfer them to a warm dish and set aside.

Using a fork, whisk the walnut and olive oils into the caramel sauce, then taste and add a little more vinegar if you think it is needed. Use this dressing to dress the salad leaves and season lightly with salt and pepper to taste.

Arrange the salad and caramelised pears in a large shallow serving dish or on individual plates and sprinkle with the walnuts. Drizzle with the Roquefort sauce and serve at once.

Pears and blue cheese: a match made in heaven! Use your favourite blue cheese here. The caramelised pears can be prepared ahead and kept in the fridge for a couple of days.

Roasted root vegetable salad
with smoked chicken

**Serves 2 as a lunch,
or 4 as a starter**

2 sweet potatoes
3 parsnips
4 small beetroot
1/2 small celeriac
2 small red onions
Olive oil for cooking
8 garlic cloves, peeled
  and chopped
2 smoked chicken breasts,
  about 150g each
Sea salt and freshly ground
  black pepper

Dressing
1 tsp English mustard
1 tsp curry powder
2 shallots, peeled and finely
  chopped
1 tsp white wine vinegar
150ml coconut milk
80ml rapeseed oil

To finish
2 tbsp roughly chopped
  parsley

Heat the oven to 190°C/Gas 5. Peel all the vegetables and cut them into bite-sized chunks. In a large roasting tray over a medium heat, heat 2 tbsp olive oil. Add all the vegetables and turn to colour on all sides for 4–5 minutes. Sprinkle with the garlic and season well with salt and pepper. Transfer to the oven and roast for about 25 minutes until tender.

In the meantime, to make the dressing, whisk all the ingredients together in a bowl until evenly combined. Tear the smoked chicken into shreds.

Toss the chicken through the warm vegetables, then pour on the dressing and toss everything together. Transfer to a large serving dish and sprinkle with chopped parsley to serve.

This tempting warm salad is equally good as a starter or colourful lunch. The coconut dressing, with its slight hint of curry, adds a unique element. You can use leftover roast chicken or turkey in place of the smoked chicken if you like.

Violet potato and smoked eel salad with horseradish cream

Serves 4 as a lunch, or 6 as a starter

8 medium violet new potatoes
6 small red beetroot
6 small yellow beetroot
1 side of smoked eel
30g pea shoots
Sea salt and freshly ground black pepper

Horseradish cream

2 tbsp freshly grated horseradish
2 tsp horseradish sauce
300ml whipping cream, softly whipped

Dressing

1 shallot, peeled and finely chopped
2 tbsp chopped parsley
3 tbsp red wine vinegar
6 tbsp olive oil

Put the potatoes and different beetroot varieties into separate saucepans. Pour on cold water to cover, add salt and bring to the boil. Lower the heat and simmer until tender, about 20 minutes.

Meanwhile, for the horseradish cream, gently fold the fresh and bottled horseradish through the whipped cream and season with salt to taste. Cover and refrigerate until needed.

To test if the potatoes and beetroot are cooked, push a small sharp knife through to the centre; it should pass through easily. Once cooked, drain and leave until cool enough to handle, then peel. Cut the potatoes and beetroot into bite-sized wedges.

Cut the eel evenly, allowing about 3 pieces per person. To make the dressing, whisk the ingredients together and season with salt and pepper to taste.

To serve, gently toss the beetroot, potatoes and pea shoots in a bowl with the dressing. Pile the salad onto individual plates or a large platter and scatter the eel on top. Serve the horseradish cream on the side.

I tasted the finest smoked eel when I worked in Maastricht in Holland in 1999, and still enjoy it here thanks to The Dutch Eel Company, who will deliver to your home. Once you try it I'm sure you'll agree it is amazing, but don't let that stop you from substituting your own favourite smoked fish – it is lovely with smoked trout, for example. Similarly, if you cannot get violet potatoes, use another waxy variety, such as Charlotte.

Potato gnocchi with Mont d'Or

**Serves 4 as a lunch,
or 6 as a starter**

Potato gnocchi
500g floury potatoes
  (ideally Rooster)
120g plain flour, plus extra
  for dusting
2 pinches of sea salt
2 tsp mild Espelette pepper
  flakes (or use freshly
  ground white pepper
  to taste)
Olive oil for cooking
Knob of butter

To serve
100g Mont d'Or cheese
1 Gem lettuce
2 celery sticks, de-stringed
  with a peeler
Olive oil for cooking
90g bacon lardons
200ml chicken stock
  (see page 184)
40g butter
4 anchovy fillets in oil,
  drained and chopped
8 sun-dried tomato pieces
Freshly ground black pepper

To make the gnocchi, cook the whole unpeeled potatoes in boiling salted water for about 20 minutes until tender, then drain and peel. Mash the potatoes thoroughly until very smooth, then add the flour, salt and pepper and mix gently until evenly combined. Knead into a smooth ball, taking care to avoid overworking.

Divide the mixture into three and roll each portion into a long cylinder, about 2cm in diameter. Cut the rolls into 2cm lengths and roll each piece in your hands to form a small ball. Place on a clean work surface and gently push your index finger into the middle of each one to make a deep indentation (as shown overleaf).

Bring a large pot of salted water to the boil, then cook the gnocchi in 3 or 4 batches, lowering them into the boiling water. They are ready when they float to the surface; this will take 2–3 minutes. As each batch is cooked, remove with a slotted spoon to a bowl of ice-cold water to refresh, then drain on kitchen paper. (You can prepare the gnocchi ahead to this stage and keep them covered with cling film in the fridge until ready to serve.)

Have the cheese ready at room temperature. Tear the lettuce leaves in half and cut the celery into bite-sized pieces. Heat a drizzle of olive oil in a saucepan and sauté the lardons until lightly coloured. Pour in the chicken stock, bring to the boil, then add the celery and cook for 2 minutes. Stir in the butter, followed by the anchovies, sun-dried tomatoes and lettuce. Remove from the heat as soon as the lettuce has just wilted. Season with pepper to taste; the bacon and anchovies should provide enough salt.

When ready to serve, heat a little olive oil in a non-stick pan and pan-fry the gnocchi until golden, then add the butter and gently toss the gnocchi in the butter as it melts. Transfer to warmed bowls and spoon some of the cheese on top. Spoon the lettuce and bacon mixture around and over the gnocchi, along with some of the cooking juices. Serve at once.

Making gnocchi is easy, so if you haven't tried before, give this recipe a go. Mont d'Or is a lovely seasonal soft cheese from the Franche-Comté region of France, close to Switzerland, at its best from October to February. When it's not available, use any other soft cheese – even a creamy blue, such as Gorgonzola. You can top the gnocchi with the cheese and warm them through in the oven at 180°C/Gas 4 for 3 minutes before serving on a platter with the salad, as shown overleaf, if you prefer.

Olive, bacon and fennel cake

Serves 4–6

110g bacon lardons
1 tsp fennel seeds
3 medium eggs
200g plain flour
10g fresh yeast, or 7g active
   dry yeast (1 sachet)
120ml olive oil, plus a little
   extra for cooking
200ml milk
120g Gruyère, grated
80g pitted green olives

Heat the oven to 180°C/Gas 4. Line a small loaf tin with greaseproof paper (mine is 22 x 11cm and 6cm deep).

Place a non-stick frying pan over a medium heat, drizzle in a little olive oil, then add the lardons. Sauté until lightly coloured. Now add the fennel seeds and toast for about 30 seconds, then remove the pan from the heat.

In a large bowl, whisk together the eggs, flour, yeast, olive oil and milk to form a smooth batter. Add the lardons, fennel seeds, Gruyère and olives and mix until evenly incorporated.

Pour the yeast batter into the lined loaf tin and bake for about 50 minutes or until a fine wooden skewer inserted into the centre comes out clean. Leave to rest in the tin for 10 minutes, then turn out onto a wire rack and leave to cool.

This is an adaptation of a recipe from my husband's grandmother Gisele, who lives in France. She would make it for us to take on our drive back to England. It's lovely for a picnic, or with a paprika dressing (see page 28) and a salad for lunch or supper. It is also ideal as a lunchbox filler.

Seafood pasta with light curry sauce

Serves 4

12 raw king prawns in shell
12 scallops, shelled and
  cleaned
1 salmon fillet, about 160g,
  skinned
2 medium squid, cleaned,
  with tentacles
500g fresh pasta
  (good-quality bought
  or home-made,
  see page 183)
Olive oil for cooking
Sea salt and freshly
  ground black pepper

Sauce

2 tbsp olive oil
1 small onion, peeled
  and finely diced
2 tbsp mild curry powder
200ml white wine
400ml fish stock
  see page 185)
600ml double cream

To finish

Chopped parsley

To prepare the seafood, peel the prawns and slice through lengthways with a sharp knife, removing the black intestinal thread that runs along the back. If the scallops are large, cut them in two. Cut the salmon into small bite-sized chunks. Cut open the squid pouches and score the inner surface lengthways with a sharp knife, being careful not to cut right through, then score again in the opposite direction. Cut into pieces, about 3cm square. Refrigerate all the seafood until needed.

To make the sauce, heat the olive oil in a small pan, add the onion and sweat gently, without colouring, until softened and translucent. Add the curry powder and cook, stirring, for 1–2 minutes. Add the wine, bring to the boil and reduce by half, then add the fish stock. Bring to the boil and reduce by about two-thirds. Add the cream, bring back to the boil and simmer gently for 5–7 minutes until reduced and thickened to a good sauce consistency; don't let it get too thick. Season with salt and pepper to taste.

When ready to serve, bring a large pan of water to the boil to cook the pasta, and salt it well. Once boiling, add the pasta and cook until al dente. At the same time, heat a large frying pan and add a good drizzle of olive oil. Add the seafood and sear over a high heat for a minute, no more, until just cooked. Take the pan off the heat, add the curry sauce and toss to combine. Taste and adjust the seasoning.

Drain the pasta as soon as it is ready and tip into a warmed serving dish or individual bowls. Pour over the seafood sauce, toss lightly and scatter over some chopped parsley. Serve at once.

This is an excellent Saturday evening supper and you can vary the seafood according to what's available and looks most inviting at your fishmongers or supermarket fresh fish counter. Nowadays there are some wonderful ready-made fresh pastas available, but make your own if you have the time and patience... you'll find it very rewarding.

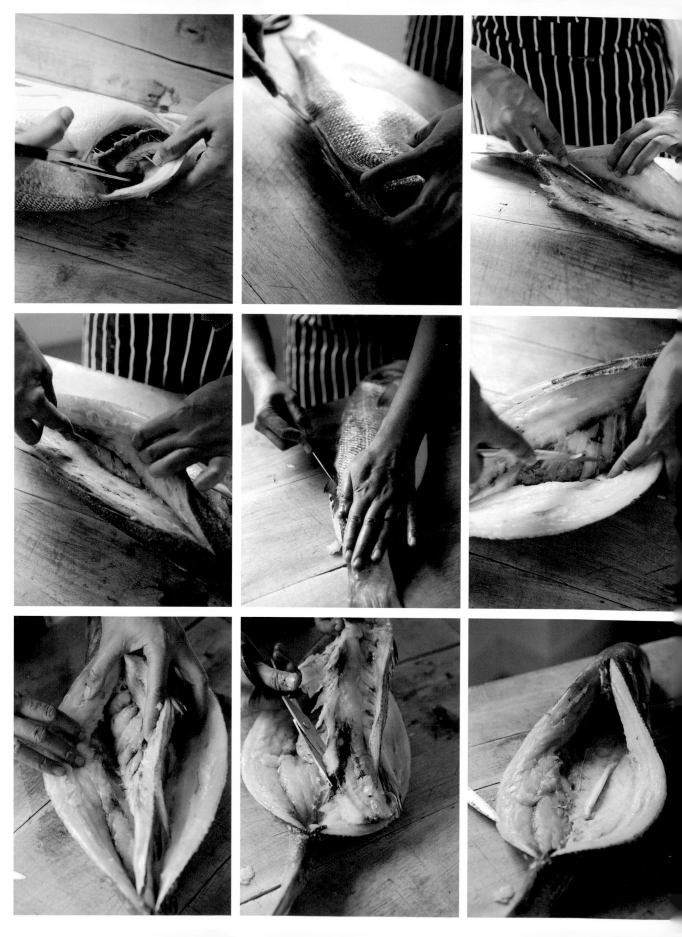

Sea bass with celeriac and fennel

Serves 6

1 whole sea bass, about
  2kg, scaled
200g celeriac, peeled
200g fennel, trimmed and
  outer layer removed
2 tsp coriander seeds
2 limes
1 tbsp olive oil
Sea salt and freshly ground
  black pepper
2 tbsp extra virgin olive oil,
  to finish

Heat the oven to 190°C/Gas 5 and put a large baking tray (one that will hold the whole fish) inside to heat up.

Using strong scissors, remove the fins and gills from the fish. Carefully make a shallow cut along the backbone, running the knife just above the bone, from head to tail, stopping 4cm before the end of the tail. Now gently use the front tip of your knife to open up the fish following the bones of the fish. Repeat on the other side, making sure you stop once you reach the belly of the sea bass and don't pierce through it. Using scissors, snip the fish bone where it connects to the head. Repeat near the tail end to release the bone (save to make stock, see page 185). You should be able to pull out all the insides, including the guts; if necessary, use scissors to cut them free. Check the fish for pin bones, removing any with kitchen tweezers. Rinse the fish and pat dry.

Using a mandoline or swivel vegetable peeler, finely slice the celeriac and fennel. Crush the coriander seeds, using a pestle and mortar. Slice the limes as thinly as possible; you want at least 15 slices.

Lay a large sheet of greaseproof paper on your work surface; it needs to be big enough to wrap around the fish. Drizzle the paper with the 1 tbsp olive oil and sprinkle with salt, pepper and a little of the crushed coriander. Arrange a thin layer of celeriac over the middle of the paper, then add a layer of fennel slices. Lay 5 lime slices on top.

Score the fish gently with a sharp knife on both sides. Season the fish cavity with salt, pepper and some crushed coriander, then place 5 lime slices inside. Place the fish on the bed of celeriac and fennel and season lightly. Lay the remaining lime slices on top of the sea bass. Scatter the remaining fennel slices over the fish, then the rest of the celeriac. Season lightly with salt, pepper and crushed coriander.

Now fold up the sides of the greaseproof and fold the edges together to enclose the fish; twist the ends to secure. Place on the hot oven tray and cook in the oven for 13–15 minutes. Carefully turn the fish over and cook for a further 13–15 minutes. Let rest for 5 minutes before opening up the paper (as shown overleaf). Drizzle with the extra virgin olive oil to serve.

I love to serve this sea bass simply with baby potatoes tossed in butter and parsley. I strongly recommend you bone out the sea bass yourself rather than get your fishmonger to do it. It's a satisfying technique to master and one that makes it so easy to portion and serve the fish (as shown overleaf).

Spatchcocked poussin with honey and pimento glaze

Serves 4

2 poussins
4 tbsp thin honey
2 tsp smoked paprika
2 large corn-on-the-cobs
Olive oil for cooking

Coleslaw

1 small cabbage, quartered
   and cored
2 carrots, peeled
1 small red onion, peeled
5 sage leaves, shredded
   (optional)
150ml mayonnaise
   (see page 183)
Squeeze of lemon juice
Sea salt and freshly ground
   black pepper

To spatchcock each poussin, using a pair of poultry shears or kitchen scissors, cut down either side of the backbone from the bottom to the top and remove it. Turn the bird over onto its front (skin side uppermost), then press down firmly on the breastbone to open the poussin out and flatten it.

Mix the honey and smoked paprika together in a small bowl, then rub all over the poussins. Place in a shallow dish and leave to marinate in the fridge for at least 2 hours.

When ready to cook, heat the oven to 190°C/Gas 5. Place the poussins in an oven tray and roast in the oven for 20–25 minutes, basting occasionally with the marinade. Bring a large pan of water to the boil for the corn.

Meanwhile, for the coleslaw, grate the cabbage and carrots and finely slice the onion. Combine in a bowl with the shredded sage, if using. Fold in the mayonnaise and season with salt, pepper and a few drops of lemon juice to taste.

Add the corn-on-the-cobs to the pan of boiling water and cook for 5–10 minutes until just tender. Heat up a griddle in the meantime. Drain the sweetcorn, pat dry and cut the cobs in half. Drizzle with a little olive oil and rub to coat the corn cobs all over. Place on the hot griddle pan for a few minutes, turning to colour on all sides.

Cut each poussin in half lengthways and serve with the coleslaw and seared corn-on-the-cob.

Opening the poussins out flat by spatchcocking helps to speed up the cooking time. Here I have roasted them, but they are also excellent cooked on the barbecue or griddle.

Roast duck with a port sauce

Serves 4

2 Gressingham ducks, about
  1.3–1.4kg each
Olive oil for cooking
4 parsnips, peeled and cut
  into large chunks
3 sweet potatoes, peeled
  and cut into large chunks
1 tsp pink peppercorns
Sea salt and freshly ground
  black pepper

Sauce
Olive oil for cooking
1 onion, peeled and cut
  into small chunks
1 carrot, peeled and cut
  into small chunks
2 celery sticks, cut into
  small chunks
100ml port
400ml chicken stock
  (see page 184)
40g butter, in pieces

Heat the oven to 190°C/Gas 5. Take out any giblets from the duck, then cut off the wing tips and neck. Remove the wishbone by running a knife down either side of the bone then pulling it out with your fingers. Keep the bones and giblets for the sauce. Cut the legs off the duck and remove the excess cartilage by bending it back until it snaps; add this to the bones.

For the sauce, put the duck bones in an oven tray and roast in the oven for 8–10 minutes. Heat a drizzle of olive oil in a large saucepan, add the vegetables and sweat over a medium heat until lightly coloured, then add the roasted bones and any giblets. Pour the port into the oven tray, stirring to deglaze, then pour onto the vegetables. Add the stock and bring to the boil, then lower the heat. Simmer gently for 20 minutes, then pass through a fine sieve into a clean pan and simmer to reduce until the sauce thickens slightly. Remove from the heat and set aside.

Meanwhile, heat a large roasting tin over a medium-high heat and add a little olive oil. Season the duck crown inside and all over with salt and pepper; season the legs too. Add the duck crown and legs to the hot tray and colour for about 5 minutes until golden all over, turning as necessary.

Add the parsnips and sweet potatoes to the tray and turn to coat in the fat. Turn the duck crown on one side and place the legs skin side down. Roast for 10 minutes, then turn the crown onto the opposite side and turn the vegetables. Roast for a further 10 minutes. Now lay the crown on its back (skin side up), turn the vegetables again, sprinkle with the pink peppercorns and roast for a final 5 minutes. Transfer the duck crown to a warm platter. Turn the legs and roast with the vegetables for a further 15–20 minutes.

To finish the sauce, reheat, if necessary, over a low heat and then whisk in the butter a piece at a time. Remove the duck breasts from the crown and cut them and the legs in two. Serve the duck with the port sauce and a green vegetable, such as cabbage or spinach.

For me, this is the best way to prepare and roast a duck – cooking the legs separately avoids the possibility of overdoing the breast or undercooking the leg meat. Roasting the vegetables in the duck fat flavours and crisps them beautifully.

Saffron lamb stew with bulgar wheat

Serves 4

1kg lamb neck fillets
2 onions, peeled
3 celery sticks, de-stringed
  with a peeler
2 carrots, peeled
Olive oil for cooking
1 tbsp plain flour
250ml Madeira
Juice of 2 oranges
2 pinches of saffron strands
$\frac{1}{2}$ red chilli
400g tin peeled whole
  tomatoes
400g tin borlotti beans,
  drained
400ml chicken stock
  (see page 184)
Sea salt and freshly ground
  black pepper

Bulgar wheat
Olive oil for cooking
1 small onion, peeled and
  chopped
650ml chicken stock
  (see page 184)
300g bulgar wheat
1 cinnamon stick

Heat the oven to 180°C/Gas 4. Trim the lamb of any excess fat, cut into large pieces and season with salt and pepper. Cut the vegetables into large chunks and set aside.

Heat a large flameproof casserole over a medium-high heat and add a drizzle of olive oil. When hot, colour the lamb in batches for a few minutes, turning to brown the pieces on all sides, then remove with a slotted spoon and set aside on a plate.

Add the vegetables to the casserole and sweat over a medium heat until lightly coloured, then return the lamb to the casserole. Stir in the flour, then add the Madeira and orange juice, stirring as you do so. Add the saffron, chilli, tinned tomatoes with their juice and the borlotti beans.

Pour on the chicken stock to cover, then season with a pinch or two each of salt and pepper. Put the lid on and transfer to the oven. Cook until the lamb is soft and tender, about 1½ hours.

For the bulgar wheat, about 20 minutes before the lamb stew will be ready, heat a little olive oil in a medium saucepan. Add the onion and sweat gently over a low heat until softened but not coloured. Meanwhile, bring the stock to a simmer in another pan and keep it at a low simmer. Add the bulgar wheat to the softened onion and sweat them together for 1–2 minutes, then add the cinnamon stick. Lower the heat and gradually add the chicken stock as you would for a risotto, a ladleful at a time, until it is all incorporated and the bulgar wheat is tender. Season with salt and pepper to taste.

Taste the lamb stew and adjust the seasoning if necessary. Serve with the bulgar wheat.

Bulgar wheat is a common storecupboard ingredient in our house.
My daughter loves it almost as much as pasta.

Steak and kidney pie with ale

Serves 4

800g Scottish beef braising
  or stewing steak
20 lamb's kidneys
Olive oil for cooking
4 onions, peeled and finely
  sliced
24 small button mushrooms
25g butter
3 tbsp plain flour
400ml London Pride or
  other good ale
600ml veal stock
  (see page 185)
5 thyme sprigs
Sea salt and freshly ground
  black pepper

Pastry lid

250g frozen ready-made puff
  pastry (keep frozen)
50g Gruyère, grated
50g Cheddar, grated

Heat the oven to 170°C/Gas 3. Cut the beef into bite-sized pieces and season with salt and pepper. Halve the kidneys, cut out the core and remove the skin, then season.

Heat a large flameproof casserole over a medium-high heat and add a generous drizzle of olive oil. When hot, colour the beef in batches for a few minutes, turning to brown the pieces on all sides, then remove with a slotted spoon and set aside on a plate. Repeat with the kidneys.

Add a little more oil to the casserole, then tip in the sliced onions and sweat over a medium heat until softened and caramelised to a rich golden brown colour. Add the mushrooms and sauté for a few minutes.

Now add the butter to the casserole and let it melt, then stir in the flour. Return the steak and kidneys to the casserole, then gradually add the ale, stirring as you do so. Bring to the boil, then stir in the veal stock, add the thyme and bring back to a simmer. Cover and cook in the oven until the beef is tender, about 1¾ hours.

Meanwhile, for the pastry lid, grate the frozen puff pastry, put into a plastic tub and keep in the freezer until needed.

When the pie filling is ready, remove the casserole from the oven and raise the heat to 190°C/Gas 5 or heat up the grill.

At the last moment, tip the grated pastry into a bowl, add all the grated cheese and quickly mix with your hands before the pastry thaws, or it will become lumpy. Spread the mixture evenly over your pie. Immediately place under the hot grill for 3–5 minutes or in the oven for 8–10 minutes until golden brown. Leave to stand for 5 minutes before serving.

Steamed Chantenay carrots drizzled with olive oil and sprinkled with smoked sea salt are an excellent accompaniment.

We all love a good comforting savoury pie. Here I've given the steak and kidney classic a twist with ale and an unusual crunchy cheese pastry lid. The puff pastry topping can be prepared ahead and kept in a tub in the freezer for a month or so.

Glazed lamb shanks with creamy mash

Serves 4

4 lamb shanks
5 star anise
2 cinnamon sticks
1 onion, peeled
1 carrot, peeled
2 celery sticks,
3 bay leaves
3 rosemary sprigs
Finely pared zest
of 1 orange
60g unsalted butter
6 tbsp thin honey
3 tbsp red wine
vinegar
Sea salt and
freshly ground
black pepper

Mash

6 medium
floury
potatoes
(ideally
Rooster)
4 tbsp crème
fraîche

Place the lamb shanks in a large cooking pot and pour on enough water to cover. Add the spices and 1 tbsp sea salt. Slowly bring to the boil.

Skim off any scum from the surface of the stock and turn the heat down to a gentle simmer. Add the vegetables, herbs and orange zest. Bring back to a low simmer and cook very gently for about 2 hours until the shanks are soft and tender. Leave to cool in the liquid.

Heat the oven to 180°C/Gas 4. Lift the lamb shanks out of the cooking pot onto a plate. Strain the stock and reserve.

Heat a large ovenproof pan over a medium-high heat and add the butter and lamb shanks. Once the butter has melted, stir in the honey. When the mixture begins to boil and caramelise, add the wine vinegar, then pour in 300ml of the reserved stock. Bring to the boil and baste the shanks with this glaze before placing in the oven.

Roast the lamb shanks for 25–30 minutes, basting every now and then with the pan juices, until they are fully glazed and shiny. If the glaze gets too thick in the pan, stir in a little more of the reserved stock.

Meanwhile, for the mash, cook the potatoes in their skins in boiling salted water for about 20 minutes until tender, then drain and peel. Mash the potatoes thoroughly, then beat in the crème fraîche with a spatula. Season with salt and pepper to taste.

Serve the glazed lamb shanks with the creamy mash and a seasonal green vegetable.

The great thing about this recipe is that you can cook the lamb shanks well ahead and keep them in the fridge for a couple of days, ready to glaze in the oven and serve. When we have this at the weekend, I often cook an extra couple of shanks to keep for an easy weekday supper.

Braised beef with sherry
and dumplings

Serves 4

1kg Scottish beef braising
  or stewing steak
2 onions, peeled
2 carrots, peeled
3 celery sticks, de-stringed
  with a peeler
Olive oil for cooking
1 tbsp plain flour
200ml sweet sherry
300ml red wine
400ml veal stock
  (see page 185)
Sea salt and freshly ground
  black pepper

Semolina dumplings
200ml milk
80g butter
90g semolina
1 medium egg
Freshly grated nutmeg

Heat the oven to 170°C/Gas 3. Cut the beef into large chunks and season with salt and pepper. Cut the vegetables into chunks and put to one side.

Heat a large flameproof casserole over a medium-high heat and add a generous drizzle of olive oil. When it is hot, colour the beef in batches for a few minutes, turning to brown the pieces on all sides, then remove with a slotted spoon and set aside on a plate.

Add the vegetables to the casserole, with a little more oil if necessary, and sweat over a medium heat until lightly coloured. Return the beef to the casserole, sprinkle with the flour and stir well. Pour in the sherry, stirring and scraping the bottom of the casserole to deglaze, then repeat with the wine. Let the liquor reduce by half, then pour in the veal stock and season with salt and pepper. Put the lid on the casserole and place in the oven. Cook for 1 hour.

Meanwhile, make the dumplings. Bring the milk and butter to the boil in a heavy-based saucepan over a medium heat. Stir in the semolina with a wooden spoon and continue to stir over the heat until the mixture forms a ball and leaves the sides of the pan clean. Remove from the heat and continue to beat with the spoon until the mixture is just warm. Mix in the egg until evenly combined and season with a generous pinch of nutmeg and salt and pepper to taste.

When the beef has been in the oven for an hour, take it out and remove the lid. Using an ice-cream scoop or a large spoon, scoop the semolina mixture into 4–6 dumplings and place on top of the stew. Put the lid back on and return to the oven. Cook for a further hour until the beef is soft and tender, removing the lid for the last 10 minutes. Leave to stand for at least 10 minutes before serving.

This all-in-one meal is comfort food at its best. The sherry adds a sweet lightness to the braise and the semolina dumplings colour and crisp up deliciously at the end of cooking. An ideal recipe to double up to serve a larger gathering.

Gammon 'pot au feu' with bread sauce

Serves 4–6

1–2 gammon shanks,
   about 1–1.5kg
Small handful of black
   peppercorns
8 cloves
6 star anise
2 cinnamon sticks
3 bay leaves
Handful of thyme sprigs
1 garlic bulb, cut in half
   horizontally
2 onions, peeled and halved
Sea salt and freshly ground
   black pepper

Pot au feu vegetables

1 small cabbage, or 18
   Brussels sprouts, trimmed
3 carrots, peeled
3 medium turnips, peeled
6 medium potatoes, peeled

Bread sauce

600ml milk
2 bay leaves
3 thyme sprigs
1/2 tsp freshly grated nutmeg
1 small onion, peeled and
   finely chopped
Knob of butter
6 slices of white bread,
   crusts removed
1 tbsp grated horseradish
   (ideally fresh, otherwise
   ready-grated from a jar),
   or to taste

Put the gammon into a deep cooking pot in which it fits quite snugly and add enough cold water to cover. Tie the spices in a piece of muslin and place in the pot with the herbs and garlic. Heat a non-stick pan, add the onion halves and pan-roast until golden brown, then add to the cooking pot. Bring to the boil, then immediately lower the heat and cook at a gentle simmer for 3–3 1/2 hours until the gammon is cooked.

Meanwhile, make the bread sauce. In a saucepan over a very low heat, gently heat the milk with the herbs and nutmeg. In another small pan, sweat the onion in a knob of butter, without colouring, until soft. Pour the milk through a strainer onto the onion. Tear the bread into pieces and add to the milk. Heat gently for a few minutes. Whisk in the horseradish and season with salt and pepper to taste. Transfer to a jug; keep warm.

To prepare the vegetables, cut the cabbage, if using, into wedges, cut the carrots into chunky slices, halve the turnips and cut the potatoes into large chunks. Either cook the vegetables separately in boiling water towards the end of the gammon cooking time to add to it once cooked, or as I prefer, add them all to the gammon pot after 3 hours and cook together; this is easier and adds extra flavour to your stock. As you add the vegetables, check the seasoning of the stock and add salt and pepper as necessary.

When ready, remove and discard the spices and herbs. Cut the gammon and vegetables into bite-sized pieces and serve on warmed plates, with some of the stock spooned over and the bread sauce on the side.

The great thing about this recipe is that on a lazy Sunday it can be left to cook on its own while you do other things. Other meats, such as ox tongue or pork hocks, can be cooked in the same way, though you would need to adjust the cooking time accordingly. Gammon shanks vary considerably in size; if small you may need to cook two.

Easy cassoulet with a herb crust

Serves 4

4 duck legs
2 carrots, peeled
1 onion, peeled
4 celery sticks, de-stringed
  with a peeler
Olive oil for cooking
4 good-quality pork
  sausages
2 garlic cloves, peeled and
  chopped
80g bacon lardons
450ml veal stock (see
  page 185) or chicken stock
  (see page 184)
2 x 400g tins flageolet or
  haricot beans, drained
4 thyme sprigs
Sea salt and freshly ground
  black pepper

Herb crust
150g dry brioche (1–2 days
  old)
10g parsley, stalks removed

Trim the duck legs, removing any excess fat, and cut them in two at the joints. Sprinkle with a large handful of sea salt and set aside for 20 minutes.

Heat the oven to 180°C/Gas 4. Cut the carrots, onion and celery into large chunks.

Dust off the excess salt from the duck legs. Heat a large non-stick frying pan over a medium-high heat and add a drizzle of olive oil. Add the duck legs and colour, turning as necessary, until golden brown all over. Place in a deep roasting tin or casserole dish with the sausages.

Add the vegetables to the frying pan and colour over a medium heat, then add the garlic and lardons. Now pour in the stock and bring to the boil. Add the beans, stir and then tip the contents of the pan over the duck legs and sausages.

Add the thyme sprigs and season generously with pepper. Cover with foil or a lid and cook in the oven for about 1¼ hours until the duck is very tender and the liquor is well reduced.

In the meantime, blitz the brioche and parsley together in a blender or food processor to crumbs.

Taste the cassoulet and adjust the seasoning as necessary. Scatter the brioche crumb mixture evenly over the surface and return to the oven, uncovered, for 2–3 minutes to crisp the topping.

An authentic cassoulet based on duck confit is wonderful if you have enough time to confit the duck yourself, but this is a great option for an easy weekend one-pot meal. You may of course prefer to cook your own beans – allow 350g dried weight and remember to put them to soak the night before.

Pear tarte tatin

Serves 4

5–6 firm, ripe Conference
   pears
125g salted butter,
   softened
5 tbsp caster sugar
1 vanilla pod, split and
   seeds scraped
2 pinches of sea salt
1 ready-rolled puff pastry
   sheet

To serve

Vanilla ice cream
   (see page 187)

Heat the oven to 180°C/Gas 4. Peel the pears, cut in half and scoop out the cores.

Take a non-stick ovenproof pan, solid-based cake tin or tatin pan, 20–22cm in diameter, and press the butter out over the base to cover it completely. Mix the caster sugar with the vanilla seeds and sprinkle evenly over the butter, then sprinkle with the salt.

Place the pear halves, rounded side down, on top of the sugar, placing them as close together as possible.

Cut out a disc of puff pastry about 2cm wider than the diameter of the pan. Lay the pastry disc on top of the pears and gently tuck in the edges of the pastry down the side of the pan.

Place the pan over a medium-high heat for about 5 minutes until the butter and sugar are melted together and bubbling, and the edges of the tatin have slightly caramelised. Transfer to the oven. Bake for 20–25 minutes until the pastry is golden brown and crisp.

As you take the tart from the oven, invert it onto a serving plate – the pears will now be sitting on top of the pastry. If you find the tart is sticking to the tin, gently reheat on the hob for a minute, return to the oven for another minute, then turn out. Serve with a scoop of vanilla ice cream.

Who can resist a tarte tatin? The salted caramel,
with its hint of vanilla, is divine.

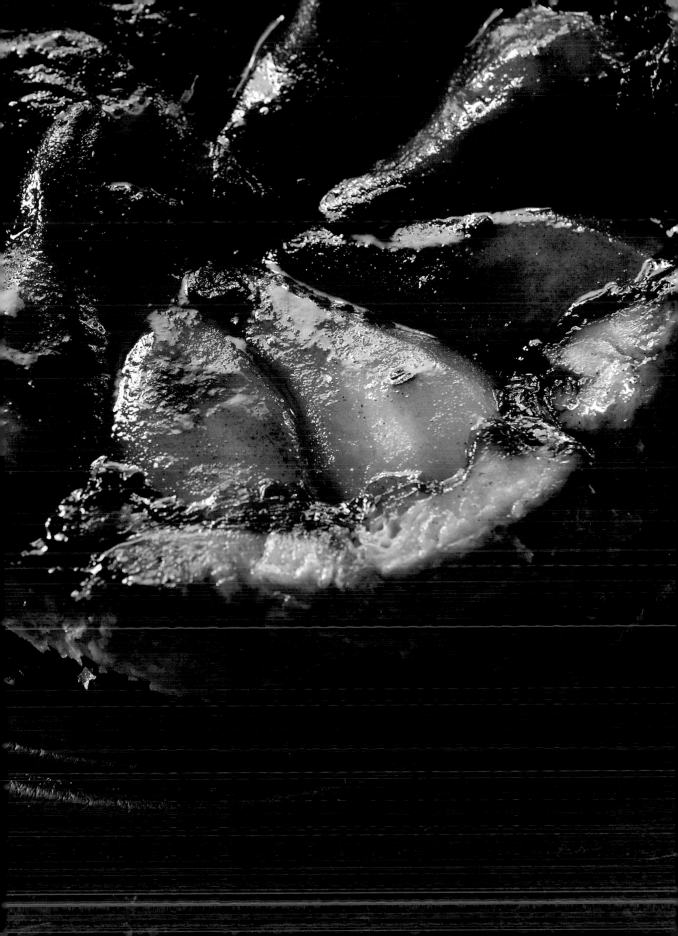

Rhubarb tarte fine

Serves 4

1 ready-rolled puff pastry
   sheet, about 35 x 25cm
Plain flour for dusting
3 sticks of rhubarb (ideally
   forced)
½ quantity of almond cream
   (see page 96)
1 medium egg yolk
1–2 tsp demerara sugar

Syrup

100ml water
100g caster sugar
1 vanilla pod, split and
   seeds scraped
Rhubarb trimmings (from
   above)

To serve

Ginger ice cream (see
   page 187) or cream

Heat the oven to 220°C/Gas 7. On a lightly floured surface, roll out the sheet of puff pastry slightly, then cut a rectangle, 34 x 16cm. Prick all over with a fork. Place in the fridge to rest while you prepare the rhubarb and syrup.

Cut the rhubarb into strips, about 12cm long and 3mm thick. For the syrup, put the water and sugar into a saucepan with the vanilla seeds and slowly bring to the boil. Add any trimmings from the rhubarb, remove from the heat and set aside to infuse and cool.

Spread a thin layer of almond cream over the pastry, about 5mm thick, leaving a 2cm clear margin around the edges. Arrange the rhubarb batons over the almond cream, overlapping them to cover it completely and pressing down lightly. Fold up the edges of the pastry to form a rim.

Brush the rhubarb with a little of the strained syrup and sprinkle evenly with demerara sugar. Bake for 15–20 minutes until the pastry is golden brown and crisp on the bottom of the tart.

Brush the rhubarb with a little more of the syrup. Serve warm with a scoop of ginger ice cream or trickle of cream. Drizzle more vanilla syrup over the ice cream.

I love to use beautiful forced rhubarb with its vivid pink, tender stalks when it becomes available during late winter. When outdoor rhubarb takes over, this simple tart is a good way to use it too – especially if you happen to have some in the garden, as we do.

Almond biscuits
with white chocolate mousse

Serves 4
(Makes 8 biscuits)

Pastry
500g plain flour, plus
  extra for dusting
150g icing sugar
Pinch of sea salt
250g butter, in pieces,
  softened
4 medium egg yolks,
  lightly beaten
50ml water

Apple compote
3 Granny Smiths or other
  crisp dessert apples
3 tbsp water
2 tbsp caster sugar
1 tsp ground cinnamon

Almond cream
120g butter, softened
120g caster sugar
120g ground almonds
2 medium eggs, beaten

To assemble
1 egg yolk, beaten, to glaze
8 split almonds

White chocolate mousse
300g good-quality white
  chocolate, in pieces
600ml double cream

To make the pastry, mix the flour, icing sugar and salt together in a bowl and rub in the butter until the mixture resembles fine crumbs. Mix in the egg yolks and enough water to form a smooth dough; do not overwork. Shape into a ball, wrap in cling film and refrigerate for 30 minutes.

For the chocolate mousse, melt the chocolate in a large bowl over a pan of barely simmering water, then take off the heat. Bring 200ml of the cream to a simmer in a pan. Whisk into the melted chocolate and continue to whisk until cool. Whip the remaining cream to soft peaks and fold into the mousse. Cover and chill until ready to serve.

For the compote, peel, quarter, core and chop the apples, then place in a saucepan with the rest of the ingredients. Cook over a medium-low heat for about 10 minutes. Allow to cool, then refrigerate until needed.

For the almond cream, whisk the butter and sugar together in a bowl until creamy. Stir in the ground almonds, then the eggs, to form a smooth paste. Cover and place in the fridge for 10 minutes to firm up slightly.

Heat the oven to 180°C/Gas 4. Divide the pastry in two, making one portion slightly larger than the other. On a lightly floured surface, roll out the smaller portion on a sheet of greaseproof paper to a 3mm thickness and cut out 8 rounds, about 8cm in diameter, for the bases. Roll out the other portion and cut 8 rounds, 10cm in diameter, for the tops.

Place a heaped teaspoon of almond cream in the centre of each of the smaller pastry rounds and make a small well in the middle. Spoon enough apple compote into the well to fill it. Brush the edges of the pastry with water. Place the larger rounds of pastry on top and press the edges down to seal, being careful to avoid trapping any air bubbles.

Brush the pastry all over with egg yolk and press half an almond on top of each biscuit. Carefully transfer to a baking sheet and bake for 8–10 minutes until golden. Leave on the baking sheet for a few minutes to firm up, then transfer to a wire rack to cool.

Serve a couple of almond-filled biscuits each, with a scoop of white chocolate mousse.

These melt-in-the-mouth biscuits are very moreish. They keep well in an airtight container and I often bake a batch at the weekend to use for midweek desserts. The chocolate mousse is delectable and one of the easiest recipes you'll ever come across.

Plum and peach crumble

Serves 4

Crumble topping
100g plain flour
90g cold unsalted butter,
   in pieces
100g caster sugar
1 tbsp desiccated coconut
2 tbsp skinned hazelnuts,
   roughly crushed

Filling
10 ripe plums
5 ripe peaches
5 tbsp demerara sugar
1 cinnamon stick
2 vanilla pods, split and
   seeds scraped

To serve
Vanilla ice cream (see
   page 187), plain yoghurt
   or crème fraîche

Heat the oven to 180°C/Gas 4. To make the crumble topping, put the flour into a large bowl and rub in the butter until the mixture looks like coarse crumbs. Mix in the sugar, coconut and crushed hazelnuts.

Spread the crumble evenly on a small baking tray lined with greaseproof paper and bake in the oven for 8–10 minutes until golden brown.

Leave to cool, then gently rub the crumble between your fingers until it is loose and crumby again. Set aside or store in an airtight container until needed if preparing well ahead.

For the filling, halve the plums and peaches and remove the stones. Cut the peach halves in two and place in a saucepan with the plums, demerara sugar, cinnamon stick and vanilla pods and seeds. Cook gently together for about 5 minutes to make a thick compote.

Divide the fruit compote between ovenproof individual bowls, removing the cinnamon stick and vanilla pods. Just before serving, sprinkle the crumble on top of the fruit and flash in the oven for 1 minute.

Serve the crumble with either a scoop of vanilla ice cream or a generous spoonful of yoghurt or crème fraîche.

During the summer I like to make the most of the abundance of fruit – berries, of course, but also the lovely stone fruits like peaches and plums. This is a great recipe for a fast dessert if, like me, you make up a big batch of crumble topping – it will keep for up to 10 days. Make a quick compote with excess fruits from your fruit bowl, top with crumble and serve with ice cream, yoghurt or crème fraîche.

Lemon cake *with lemon curd*

Serves 8

200g unsalted butter,
  softened, plus extra
  for greasing
Plain flour for dusting
300g caster sugar
6 medium eggs, separated
200g white self-raising flour
100g wholemeal self-raising
  flour
2 level tsp baking powder
Finely grated zest and juice
  of 6 lemons (250ml juice)

Lemon curd
Juice of 4 lemons
3 medium egg yolks,
  plus 1 whole egg
160g caster sugar
100g butter

To serve (optional)
Clotted cream

Heat the oven to 170°C/Gas 3. Lightly grease the base and sides of a 20–22cm spring-release cake tin, about 6cm deep, and dust with flour.

In a large bowl, beat the butter and sugar together thoroughly until pale and creamy, then beat in the egg yolks, one at a time. Sift the flour and baking powder together, then fold into the mixture, alternately with the lemon zest and juice.

In another large bowl, whisk the egg whites to soft peaks, then carefully fold into the cake mixture, using a large metal spoon or spatula.

Pour the mixture into the prepared cake tin and bake in the oven for 50–60 minutes or until a skewer inserted into the centre comes out clean. Leave the cake to rest in the tin for 5 minutes, then turn out onto a wire rack and leave to cool.

To make the lemon curd, whisk the lemon juice, egg yolks, whole egg and sugar together in a heavy-based saucepan over a very low heat until the mixture thickens; don't let it come to the boil – take the pan off the heat as necessary if the mixture seems to be getting too hot. Remove from the heat and whisk in the butter. Allow to cool.

Either serve the cake sliced with a dollop of lemon curd on the side, or split the cake into two layers and sandwich together with lemon curd. Serve with clotted cream for total indulgence.

Making lemon cake is always a weekend affair with my daughter, because it is her favourite too. I like to use a mixture of white and wholemeal flours, but for an even lighter cake use just white self-raising flour. Served with raspberries or wild strawberries and clotted cream, this is the perfect summer dessert.

Dark chocolate brownie

Serves 8–10

220g good-quality dark
  chocolate (minimum 60%
  cocoa solids), in pieces
180g unsalted butter,
  softened
5 medium eggs
200g soft brown sugar
80g plain flour
Icing sugar for dusting

Melt the chocolate in a large bowl set over a pan of gently simmering water. Take off the heat, add the soft butter and stir until melted and the mixture is smooth. Set aside to cool slightly.

In another large bowl, beat the eggs and sugar together thoroughly, using an electric whisk, for about 10 minutes until mousse-like, then fold into the chocolate mixture. Now sift the flour over the mixture and gently fold in. Cover the bowl and leave the mixture to rest in the fridge for 30 minutes before baking.

Heat the oven to 190°C/Gas 5. Line a shallow baking tin, about 23 x 33cm, with greaseproof paper. Spoon the mixture into the tin and gently spread it into the corners with the back of the spoon. Bake for 12 minutes until crusted on top but still soft inside.

Leave in the tin for 10 minutes, then carefully transfer the brownie to a wire rack to cool. Cut into squares and dust with icing sugar to serve.

I love dark chocolate and this recipe is so easy and foolproof that it's become a firm favourite. I use the same mixture to make chocolate fondants with melting centres: fill ovenproof cups or metal rings, 6cm in diameter and 4cm high, set on a baking tray, and bake at 190°C/Gas 5 for 5–6 minutes. These are delicious with pistachio ice cream (see page 187), or a white chocolate crème anglaise (see page 186).

A Time
for Friends

Jerusalem artichoke and parsley soups

Serves 6 as a starter

Jerusalem artichoke soup

1kg Jerusalem artichokes
2 tbsp olive oil
2 onions, peeled and thinly sliced
2 garlic cloves, peeled, halved and germ removed
1.2 litres chicken stock (see page 184)
200ml single cream (optional)
Sea salt and freshly ground black pepper

Parsley soup

3 large bunches of flat-leaf parsley, about 120g each
650ml water
180ml double cream
100g salted butter

To serve

200ml vegetable oil, for deep-frying
2 Jerusalem artichokes (reserved from above)
Olive oil for cooking
30 whelks or snails, cleaned
1 shallot, peeled and finely chopped
2 garlic cloves, peeled and finely chopped
40g butter
6 parsley leaves

Wine suggestion:
A Viognier from Côtes du Rhône or USA

For the artichoke soup, set aside 2 Jerusalem artichokes. Peel and roughly chop the rest. Heat the olive oil in a saucepan, add the onions and sweat over a medium heat for about 5 minutes to soften without colouring. Add the chopped artichokes with the garlic, pour on the chicken stock and bring to the boil. Lower the heat and simmer for about 20 minutes until the artichokes are cooked. Blitz the soup in a blender until smooth and season with salt and pepper to taste. Return to the pan and set aside.

To make the parsley soup, pull the parsley leaves from their stems and set aside. Put the parsley stems in a large saucepan with the water. Bring to the boil, lower the heat and simmer for 15 minutes. Pass this parsley stock through a sieve into a bowl and reserve; discard the parsley stems.

Add the parsley leaves to a pan of boiling salted water and blanch for a few seconds, then scoop out and refresh in cold water. Drain and return to the boiling water. Simmer for 10 minutes. Drain the leaves in a sieve, pressing out any excess water. Heat the cream, just to the boil.

Put the drained parsley leaves in a blender and blitz, gradually adding the hot cream, until smooth. Tip the purée into a saucepan and add enough of the parsley stock to give a good soup consistency.

For the garnish, heat the oil in a deep, heavy saucepan. Peel the reserved 2 Jerusalem artichokes and slice thinly, using a mandoline or vegetable peeler. Deep-fry the slices, in batches, for a minute or so until crispy. Drain on kitchen paper and set aside.

Heat a large frying pan and add a small drizzle of olive oil. Add the whelks, toss gently, then add the shallot and garlic and cook for 30 seconds. Add the butter, toss the whelks again and season with salt and pepper.

To serve, reheat the artichoke soup and stir in the cream, if using. Reheat the parsley soup and whisk in the butter. Pour the soups simultaneously into either side of warm soup bowls and put the whelks in the centre. Top each serving with a few deep fried artichoke slices and a parsley leaf.

The sweetness of Jerusalem artichokes and earthy tones of parsley complement each other so well in this starter. The whelks complete it for me, but if you can't get them, or snails, finish the soups with crisp-fried squid, or for a vegetarian option, omit the garnish and use vegetable stock.

Home-made ricotta with pickled
cucumber and radishes

Serves 6 as a starter

Ricotta
4 litres full-fat milk
90ml lemon juice (about
   2 lemons)
2 tsp fine salt

Pickled vegetables
200ml white wine vinegar
100ml water
60g sugar
1 cucumber
12 pink radishes

To serve
60g mixed salad leaves
2 tbsp rapeseed oil
Sea salt and freshly ground
   black pepper
Ciabatta or country-style
   bread, thinly sliced and
   toasted

Wine suggestion:
A Grüner Veltliner from Austria

To make the ricotta, pour the milk into a wide heavy-based saucepan and add the lemon juice and salt. Place over a medium-low heat and cook very gently, stirring every now and then to make sure it doesn't catch on the bottom of the pan; do not allow to boil. Cook for 25–30 minutes, lowering the heat if necessary, until the milk has completely separated. The milk solids will float to the surface, leaving a very thin watery milk underneath.

Carefully pour the mixture into a large muslin-lined sieve over the sink to drain off the liquid. (Or divide between two smaller muslin-lined sieves.) Now twist the corners of the muslin gently together and tie to form a bag. Suspend the bag(s) over a bowl in the fridge overnight to allow the excess liquid to drain away. Before serving, twist the muslin to shape the ricotta within into a ball.

To prepare the pickling juice, put the wine vinegar, water and sugar into a saucepan and bring to the boil, making sure the sugar has fully dissolved; set aside.

Cut the cucumber in half lengthways, then slice thinly with a swivel vegetable peeler. Cut the radishes into small wedges. Gently warm the pickling liquor, then add the cucumber and radishes and leave to macerate for 1 minute. Remove the cucumber slices, leaving the radishes in the liquor for another 2 minutes. Drain, reserving 1 tbsp of the pickling liquor. Roll the cucumber slices decoratively.

To serve, toss the salad leaves in the rapeseed oil and reserved 1 tbsp pickling liquor. Arrange the salad leaves, pickled vegetables and ricotta on a platter. Add a sprinkling of salt and pepper. Serve with the warm toast.

This is so simple, yet so impressive, you have got to give it a try! It will keep in the fridge for up to 4 days but I doubt that it will be around for that long.

Asparagus with deep-fried pancetta-crumbed egg

Serves 6 as a starter

30 asparagus spears
8 medium eggs, plus
  2 beaten eggs for coating
150g pancetta
100g Japanese panko
  breadcrumbs
4 tbsp plain flour
20ml truffle oil
10ml rapeseed oil
30g rocket leaves
500ml vegetable oil for
  deep-frying
1 tsp white wine vinegar
20g Parmesan, finely grated
Sea salt and freshly ground
  black pepper

Wine suggestion:
A Pinot Blanc from Alsace or
Pinot Bianco from Italy

Snap off the tough ends of the asparagus, leaving about 11cm long spears. Add the asparagus to a pan of boiling salted water and cook for 2–3 minutes. Drain and refresh in iced salted water, then drain and set aside.

Gently place the 8 eggs in a pan of boiling salted water and cook for no more than 5 minutes. (I cook the extra couple in case of breakages!) Remove and cool in iced water, then carefully peel away the shells.

Add the pancetta to a pan of cold water, bring to the boil, then leave to cool in the water. Drain and pat dry. Finely dice the pancetta and mix with the breadcrumbs. Scatter on a small tray. Have the beaten eggs and flour ready in separate bowls.

Dip the peeled eggs into the flour to coat lightly, then in the beaten egg and finally in the crumb mix (as shown overleaf). Coat the eggs a second time with the beaten egg and crumb mix. Keep on a tray in the fridge until ready to cook.

When ready to serve, heat the grill to medium-high. Mix the truffle and rapeseed oils together. Put the rocket into a bowl.

Heat the oil for deep-frying in a deep, heavy pan to 175°C. Deep-fry the crumb-coated eggs in two batches: add them to the oil and cook for 1 minute until nice and golden, then drain on kitchen paper.

Meanwhile, lay the asparagus spears on a tray, drizzle with some of the truffle oil mixture and season with salt and pepper. Place under the grill for 40 seconds to warm through. Dress the rocket with the wine vinegar, remaining truffle oil mix and some salt and pepper.

Dip the ends of the asparagus spears in the Parmesan to coat (as shown overleaf) and arrange in a criss-cross fashion on individual plates. Carefully halve the deep-fried eggs and arrange an egg on each plate. Scatter the rocket salad over and around the asparagus. Serve at once.

The asparagus season is one of my favourite times of the year. I love this vegetable in all its guises – from plump green English spears to the white and wild types. Grilled and lightly coated with grated Parmesan, asparagus spears are delicious dipped into deep-fried soft eggs.

Wild mushroom risotto with
cep cappuccino

Serves 6 as a starter

2 handfuls of trompette
  mushrooms
2 handfuls of oyster
  mushrooms
1 handful of shimeji
  mushrooms
5 medium ceps
Olive oil for cooking
1 white onion, peeled
  and finely chopped
700ml chicken or
  vegetable stock
  (see page 184)
300g risotto rice
100ml dry white wine
40g butter
60g mascarpone
40g Parmesan, freshly
  grated
Sea salt and freshly
  ground black pepper

Cep cappuccino
30g dried ceps (or other
  dried wild mushrooms)
300ml double cream
300ml milk

Wine suggestion:
A slightly oaked Chardonnay
from Australia or South Africa

Clean all of the mushrooms, keeping them separate. Shred the trompettes and oyster mushrooms; trim off the base of the shimejis; slice the ceps. For the cappuccino, blitz the dried ceps to a powder in a blender or small food processor.

Heat a medium saucepan over a medium heat and add a good drizzle of olive oil. Add the onion and sweat for about 5 minutes to soften without colouring. Meanwhile, bring the stock to the boil in another pan and keep it at a low simmer. Add the rice to the onion and cook, stirring, for a minute or two. Pour in the wine and let it bubble to reduce right down.

Now start adding the stock, a ladleful at a time, stirring occasionally and allowing each addition to be absorbed before adding the next. Continue until the stock is all added and the rice is cooked, but with a slight bite; this should take 15–20 minutes.

Meanwhile, heat a large frying pan and add a drizzle of olive oil. Add the ceps and sauté for a minute or two until golden, adding a knob of butter as they colour. Tip into a tray and keep warm. Repeat with the remaining mushrooms and then combine them. Season with salt and pepper to taste.

For the cep cappuccino, put the cream, milk and cep powder into a saucepan and bring to a gentle simmer. Take off the heat and season with salt and pepper. Set aside.

When the risotto is ready, take the pan off the heat and fold in the mascarpone and Parmesan. Season with salt and pepper to taste.

Ladle the risotto into warm deep plates or bowls and top with the sautéed mushrooms. Blitz the cappuccino with a handheld stick blender to make it thick and frothy, then pour around the risotto. Serve immediately.

This is one of my favourite risottos. Once you have the knack of cooking a risotto, it is easy to vary the flavouring ingredients. To turn this into a supper, add sliced cooked chicken breast or sautéed lardons. If you can't source these particular mushrooms, just use a mixture of whatever you can find.

Cod brandade in squid ink

Serves 4 as a starter

500g cod or pollock fillet
2 medium potatoes
    (unpeeled)
600ml milk
200ml water
1 garlic bulb, cut in half
    horizontally
100ml olive oil
2 tsp truffle oil
70g Japanese panko
    breadcrumbs
50g squid ink
100g plain flour
2 medium eggs, beaten
400ml vegetable oil for
    deep-frying
Sea salt and freshly ground
    black pepper

Avocado sauce
2 ripe avocados
Juice of 1 lime, or to taste
Few drops of Tabasco

Wine suggestion:
A light Chenin Blanc from
the Loire valley, or an Albariño
from Spain

Lay the fish on a tray, sprinkle generously with sea salt, turning to coat both sides, then cover with cling film and refrigerate for 30 minutes.

Rinse the fish to remove the salt. Add the potatoes to a pan of salted water and cook until tender. Drain and leave to cool slightly.

Meanwhile, place the fish in a wide saucepan with the milk, water and garlic. Poach gently until cooked, about 5 minutes, then remove from the heat. Lift out the fish onto a board and remove any bones and skin. Strain and reserve 200ml of the poaching liquor.

Peel and mash the potatoes, then place in a blender with the cooked fish. Blend until smooth, add the reserved poaching liquor and blitz again until smooth. Now add the olive and truffle oils and blitz briefly to combine. Transfer to a bowl, cover and refrigerate for 20 minutes or so to firm up.

To make the sauce, halve, peel and stone the avocados. Roughly cut them up and place in a blender. Blitz until smooth, seasoning with the lime juice, Tabasco, salt and pepper to taste.

Put the breadcrumbs into a blender with the squid ink and blitz briefly to make a black crumb mix. Tip into a bowl. Put the flour and eggs into separate bowls. Heat the oil in a deep-fryer or other suitable deep, heavy pan.

Shape the chilled brandade mixture into bite-sized balls. One at a time, dip into the flour to dust, then into the egg and finally in the black crumb mix to coat all over. Fry the brandade balls in the hot oil, in batches, for 1–2 minutes until firm. Remove and drain on kitchen paper. Serve at once, with the avocado sauce.

These crisp little brandade balls are lovely served at the start of a meal with drinks. I also use them to dress up other fish dishes. Conveniently, the brandade mixture can be shaped and frozen, then coated in the crumbs and deep-fried to serve.

Crayfish and mango salad

1 ripe mango
2 ripe avocados
180g cooked peeled
   crayfish tails
2 spring onions, trimmed
   and finely sliced
10 basil leaves, shredded
Few drops of Tabasco,
   to taste
Sea salt and freshly ground
   black pepper

Lime confit
3 limes
100g caster sugar
100ml water

Dressing
1 ripe mango
1 bunch of basil, leaves only
100ml extra virgin olive oil
Juice of I lime, or to taste
Few drops of Tabasco,
   to taste

To serve
60g rocket leaves
2 tbsp rapeseed oil
2 tsp lime juice
Thinly sliced focaccia,
   toasted

First prepare the lime confit. Finely peel the zest from the limes with a swivel vegetable peeler and slice it finely into julienne strips. (Save the limes to squeeze the juice for the dressing and to dress the rocket.) Place the lime zest in a small saucepan. Add enough cold water to cover, bring to the boil, then drain. Repeat this process twice more. Put the sugar and water into another saucepan and slowly bring to the boil, making sure the sugar is fully dissolved. Add the blanched zests and bring to the boil. Take off the heat and leave to cool.

To make the dressing, peel the mango and cut the flesh from the stone. Place in a blender with the basil and blitz until smooth. Transfer to a bowl and stir in the extra virgin oil. Add the lime juice and Tabasco to taste, and a few turns of the pepper mill to give the right balance of flavourings.

For the salad, peel the mango and cut the flesh into 1cm cubes, discarding the stone. Peel, halve and stone the avocados and cut the flesh into 1cm cubes. In a large bowl, toss together the avocados, mango and crayfish tails. Add the sliced spring onions, shredded basil leaves and 2 tbsp of the cooled lime confit. Season with Tabasco, salt and pepper to taste and toss together gently.

Divide the salad between individual metal ring moulds placed on serving plates. Press gently, then remove the rings. Toss the rocket leaves with the rapeseed oil, lime juice and some salt and pepper. Arrange on top of the crayfish salad. Spoon the dressing around the edge. Serve with warm toasted focaccia.

Wine suggestion:
An aromatic Gewürztraminer
from Alsace or New Zealand

We tend to make this at the restaurant with freshly cooked lobsters, but crayfish are excellent too, and even better if they are freshly cooked. A wonderful summer dish to impress your friends.

Chicken livers with white onion purée

Serves 6

400g chicken livers
6 tbsp olive oil
2 shallots, peeled and finely
  chopped
2 tbsp sherry vinegar
2 tsp chopped tarragon
2 tsp chopped flat-leaf
  parsley
Sea salt and freshly ground
  black pepper

Onion purée
1 tbsp olive oil
1kg white onions, peeled
  and finely sliced
1 tbsp salted butter
150ml milk

Onion crisps
1 white onion, peeled and
  thinly sliced
200ml milk
150ml vegetable oil for
  deep-frying
2 tbsp plain flour
150ml vegetable oil

To serve
6 slices of brioche, cut
  1.5cm thick
50g mixed salad leaves

Wine suggestion:
A juicy Gamay from
Beaujolais

First make the onion purée. Heat the olive oil in a large pan over a medium heat. Add the sliced onions and sweat without colouring for about 5 minutes. Add the butter and cook for a further 3 minutes. Add the milk, bring to the boil and cook gently for a further 5 minutes. Transfer to a blender and blitz until very smooth. Return to the pan and set aside.

For the onion crisps, put the sliced onion into a bowl, pour on the milk and leave to soak for about 5 minutes. Remove and pat dry on kitchen paper. Heat the oil in a heavy-based pan. Toss the onion slices in the flour to coat, then fry in the hot oil in 3 or 4 batches until golden and crispy. Drain on kitchen paper and set aside; keep warm.

Trim the chicken livers of any sinews and season with salt and pepper. Heat a non-stick frying pan over a medium-high heat and add a drizzle of olive oil. Add the chicken livers to the pan and cook, turning, for about 2 minutes until golden on both sides. Remove the livers and set aside on a plate; keep warm.

Add a little more olive oil to the pan, then toss in the shallots and cook for a minute or two. Add the sherry vinegar, stirring to deglaze, then take off the heat and stir in the rest of the olive oil and the herbs to make a dressing. Season with salt and pepper to taste.

Toast the brioche slices on both sides and reheat the onion purée if necessary. Place a slice of toasted brioche on each plate and spread a thick layer of onion purée on top. Cut each chicken liver into 4 or 5 pieces and place on the onion purée. Dress the salad with a little of the shallot dressing, then arrange around the livers. Add a few crispy onion pieces and drizzle more dressing onto the livers and salad. Serve immediately.

This is my preferred way to eat chicken or even rabbit livers; it also works very well with calf's liver. I like to cook liver pink-medium to ensure a succulent, juicy texture.

Pollock poached in spiced red wine

Serves 6

6 pollock fillets, about
  170g each
400ml veal stock
  (see page 185)
25g butter
Sea salt and freshly ground
  black pepper

Spiced red wine
2 cinnamon sticks
10 cloves
1 tbsp coriander seeds
1 tbsp cumin seeds
5 cardamom pods
1 litre red wine

**Jerusalem artichoke
  purée**
400g Jerusalem artichokes
50g butter
100ml double cream

Balsamic salsify
6 sticks of salsify
1 lemon, halved
200ml good-quality thick
  balsamic vinegar

To garnish
Micro cress or watercress
Salsify crisps (optional),
  see below

Wine suggestion:
A spicy Syrah from Australia
or Côtes du Rhône

For the spiced red wine, heat a heavy-based saucepan over a medium heat, then add the spices and toast for a minute or two to release their aromas. Pour in the red wine, bring to the boil and take off the heat. Set aside to infuse and cool, then strain through a fine sieve. This spiced wine will keep in the fridge for up to 2 weeks.

For the purée, peel the Jerusalem artichokes, place in a saucepan and cover with cold water. Add a generous pinch of salt, bring to the boil, then lower the heat and simmer for about 10 minutes until tender. Drain, then return to the pan and put back over a medium heat to dry out for a minute. Add the butter and let it turn a nutty brown colour. Add the cream and heat through. Transfer to a blender and blitz until smooth. Scrape into a bowl and season with salt and pepper to taste.

Simmer 250ml of the spiced wine in a pan until reduced by half, then add the veal stock and continue to reduce over a medium heat to a sauce consistency, about 15 minutes. Take the sauce off the heat and whisk in the butter; keep warm.

To prepare the salsify, peel, then immediately immerse in a pan of cold water with the lemon halves. Add a generous pinch of salt and bring to the boil. Lower the heat and simmer until just tender when tested with a knife. Drain the salsify and place in a pan with the balsamic vinegar. Bring to a simmer and cook for 2–3 minutes until richly glazed.

Pour the rest of the spiced wine into a wide pan and bring to a bare simmer over a low heat. Add the pollock fillets, making sure they are completely immersed. Poach very gently until just cooked, about 4–5 minutes. Meanwhile, warm the Jerusalem artichoke purée.

Place spoonfuls of the Jerusalem artichoke purée on warmed serving plates and drag a spoon decoratively through the purée. Arrange a pile of salsify on each plate. Place a pollock fillet alongside and garnish with cress. Spoon the sauce over the fish, finish with salsify crisps, if you wish, and serve.

This dish has been tried and tested on my husband so many times that when it appeared on the à la carte menu at Le Gavroche all he could do was smile and shake his head. The salsify crisps are optional but easy: shave wafer-thin strips of salsify with a swivel peeler and deep-fry in hot oil for a couple of minutes, then drain on kitchen paper.

Steamed turbot with pearl barley

Serves 6

6 turbot fillets, about
  170g each
20ml medium dry Muscat
  wine
Sea salt and freshly ground
  black pepper

Pearl barley
1 tbsp olive oil
2 shallots, peeled and
  finely chopped
650ml chicken stock
  (see page 184)
200g pearl barley
100ml dry white wine
50g butter

Rhubarb
2 sticks of rhubarb
  (ideally forced)
150g caster sugar
300ml water

Raisin mustard sabayon
4 medium egg yolks
2 tsp sugar
200ml medium dry Muscat
  wine
1 tbsp raisin mustard

To finish
Micro-cress or watercress

Wine suggestion:
A fragrant Roussanne/
Marsanne from USA,
Australia or Côtes du Rhône

Put the turbot fillets in a shallow dish, drizzle with the 20ml wine and set aside until ready to cook.

For the pearl barley, heat the olive oil in a medium saucepan and sweat the shallots over a medium heat for a few minutes to soften without colouring. Meanwhile, heat the chicken stock in another pan and keep it at a low simmer. Add the pearl barley to the softened shallot and cook, stirring, for a minute. Pour in the wine and cook for another minute. Now add the hot stock, a ladleful at a time, stirring gently as you would a risotto and allowing each addition to be absorbed before adding the next. Continue until the pearl barley is tender and most of the stock has been absorbed (there should be some liquor); this will take about 20 minutes. Season with salt and pepper, take off the heat and stir in the butter.

Slice the rhubarb on an angle into 1cm thick slices. Dissolve the sugar in the water in a saucepan over a medium heat, then bring to the boil. Drop the rhubarb pieces into the boiling syrup, then take the pan off the heat. Set aside to allow the rhubarb to cook in the residual heat of the syrup for 1 minute. Meanwhile, bring some water to the boil in a steamer.

To make the sabayon, whisk the egg yolks, sugar and wine together in a large heatproof bowl over a pan of simmering water until very thick and pale. Remove from the heat and whisk for a few more minutes, then fold in the raisin mustard.

Season the turbot fillets with salt and pepper. Place in the steamer and drizzle over the wine from the dish. Cover and steam for 2–3 minutes until just cooked. Drain the rhubarb.

To serve, spoon the pearl barley into warmed deep serving plates, adding some of the liquor. Arrange the rhubarb over the barley, then place the fish on top. Spoon the sabayon over the fish and finish with cress.

Turbot is undoubtedly one of my favourite fish, and one of the most expensive, though you can substitute another meaty fish, such as brill or monkfish here. I like to serve the dish with a steamed green vegetable, such as spinach or sprouting broccoli, tossed in a little olive oil with a squeeze of lemon and some salt and pepper.

Chicken with fennel and tomatoes

Serves 6

6 corn-fed boneless chicken
    breasts (with skin), about
    150g each
4 sun-dried tomato halves,
    finely chopped
2 tsp thyme leaves
Olive oil for cooking
6 baby fennel bulbs, about
    300g, feathery fronds
    reserved to finish
2 tsp fennel seeds, crushed
100ml dry white wine
300ml chicken stock
    (see page 184)
30 small Jersey Royals
    (or other new potatoes),
    peeled
25g salted butter
2 tsp lemon juice
2 tbsp extra virgin olive oil
Sea salt and freshly ground
    black pepper

Fennel purée
500g fennel
3 tbsp olive oil
50ml Pernod
200ml chicken stock
    (see page 184)
80ml double cream

Wine suggestion:
A white Grenache from Spain
or France

Heat the oven to 180°C/Gas 4. Gently work your fingers under the skin of each chicken breast to form a pocket. Mix the sun-dried tomatoes with the thyme leaves and a pinch of salt. Push the mixture under the chicken skin and gently spread it out, without tearing the skin.

Heat a sauté pan over a medium-high heat and add a drizzle of olive oil. Add the baby fennel bulbs and turn to colour on all sides. Add the fennel seeds and season with salt and pepper. Pour in the wine, let bubble to reduce by half, then add the chicken stock. Turn the heat down, lay a round of greaseproof paper over the fennel and cook gently until tender, about 10 minutes. Leave to cool in the liquid.

To make the fennel purée, thinly slice the fennel, including any feathery fronds. Heat a sauté pan over a medium-high heat and drizzle in the olive oil. Add the fennel and cook, stirring, for about 5 minutes. Add the Pernod and let bubble to reduce for 2 minutes. Pour in the chicken stock and cook for 3–5 minutes until the fennel is very soft. Add the cream and bring to a simmer. Transfer to a blender and blitz until smooth. Return to the pan, season with salt and pepper to taste and set aside.

Add the potatoes to a pan of boiling salted water and cook for about 8 minutes until two-thirds cooked (they should have a little resistance when pierced with the tip of a knife).

Meanwhile, heat a large non-stick ovenproof frying pan over a medium-high heat and add a drizzle of olive oil. Season the chicken breasts with salt and pepper, place skin side down in the pan and colour for 1 minute. Turn and colour the other side for a minute, then add the butter. Place in the oven for about 8 minutes until cooked through, turning halfway.

Meanwhile, drain the potatoes. Place on a baking tray, drizzle with olive oil, season with salt and pepper and turn to coat. Bake in the oven for about 7 minutes until golden and crispy, tossing lightly halfway through.

Once the chicken breasts are cooked, leave them to rest in a warm place for 5 minutes before serving. Gently reheat the fennel purée.

Take the fennel out of its liquid. Bring the liquid to the boil, add the lemon juice, then the extra virgin olive oil and check the seasoning. Return the fennel to the sauce and reheat gently. Slice the chicken breasts.

Put a generous spoonful of fennel purée on each warm plate and arrange the chicken and fennel on top with the potatoes. Froth the sauce with a handheld stick blender, pour over the chicken and fennel and serve, garnished with more fennel purée and sprigs of the reserved fennel fronds. Serve with sautéed spinach or other greens.

Stuffed chicken legs with pea ragoût

Serves 6

6 whole chicken legs
  (thighs and drumsticks)
Olive oil for cooking
25g butter, softened
Sea salt and freshly ground
  black pepper

Stuffing

5 Cumberland sausages,
  about 60g each
100g wild mushrooms,
  cleaned
60g dry white breadcrumbs
1 tbsp chopped rosemary
1 tbsp lemon thyme leaves
3 medium eggs, beaten

Pea ragoût

18 new potatoes, scrubbed
18 baby onions, peeled
18 Chantenay carrots,
  scrubbed and halved
  lengthways
400g freshly podded peas
200g smoked bacon lardons
600ml chicken stock
  (see page 184)
80g unsalted butter,
  in pieces
2 Gem lettuce, roughly
  sliced

Wine suggestion:
A smooth Merlot from
Bordeaux or New Zealand

Heat the oven to 180°C/Gas 4. Carefully bone out the whole chicken legs, without piercing through the skin (as shown overleaf). Season lightly with salt and pepper.

For the stuffing, skin the sausages and roughly chop the wild mushrooms. Heat a drizzle of olive oil in a frying pan over a medium-high heat, add the mushrooms and sauté for a minute or two until tender. In a large bowl, mix the sausagemeat and mushrooms with the breadcrumbs, herbs and enough beaten egg to bind the stuffing.

Spoon the stuffing into the chicken legs to fill. Tear off 6 rectangles of foil large enough to wrap around the chicken legs. Brush the foil with the soft butter and sprinkle with salt and pepper. Place a stuffed chicken leg on each piece of foil and roll firmly to enclose, twisting the ends to seal.

Heat a frying pan over a high heat and add a little olive oil. Put the foil-wrapped chicken legs in the pan and cook for about 30 seconds, then turn and repeat to seal them on both sides (this prevents the stuffing from bursting out). Transfer to an oven tray and place in the oven for 15 minutes or until cooked through, turning halfway through cooking.

Meanwhile, prepare the ragoût. Add the potatoes to a pan of boiling salted water and cook for 12–15 minutes until tender; drain, peel away the skins and set aside. Blanch the baby onions, carrots and peas separately in boiling salted water until just tender. Drain and refresh in cold water, then drain well.

Once the chicken legs are cooked, leave them to rest in a warm place for 3 minutes before serving.

Heat a sauté pan over a medium-high heat, add a drizzle of olive oil and fry the lardons until golden. Pour in the chicken stock and let bubble to reduce by half, then stir in the butter to give a glossy sauce consistency.

To serve, add the cooked vegetables to the sauce and heat through, then take off the heat. Fold in the lettuce. Unwrap and slice the chicken. Divide the ragoût between warm plates, top with the sliced stuffed chicken and serve at once.

Stuffed and cooked in foil, the chicken is wonderfully moist and tender and the spring vegetable ragoût is a lovely accompaniment. You just need to bone out the chicken legs, which isn't that difficult.

Boning out a chicken leg for stuffing

First locate the end of the thigh bone and cut it free from the surrounding connective tissue, using a sharp, thin filleting knife. Now carefully scrape down the thigh bone to gradually release it from the meat.

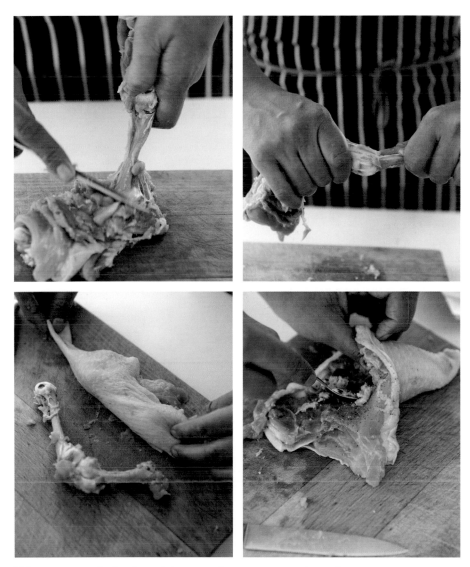

When you reach the knee joint, continue to scrape along the drumstick bone to release it from the meat until you reach the end, then twist the bone to pull it out from the meat. You will now be able to stuff the cavity of the fully boned-out leg.

Guinea fowl with Romanesco couscous

Serves 6

6 boneless guinea fowl
    breasts (with skin)
Olive oil for cooking
2 shallots, peeled and finely
    chopped
1 tbsp caster sugar
2 tbsp white wine vinegar
400ml brown chicken stock
    (see page 184)
50g salted butter
Sea salt and freshly ground
    black pepper

Shallot purée
2 tbsp olive oil
500g shallots, peeled and
    roughly sliced
2 tbsp caster sugar
50g butter
2–3 tbsp double cream,
    heated (to thin, if needed)

Romanesco couscous
1 Romanesco cauliflower
1 small standard cauliflower
210ml water
100g couscous
20ml extra virgin olive oil

Wine suggestion:
A Pinot Gris

To make the shallot purée, heat the 2 tbsp olive oil in a large pan over a medium heat. Add the sliced shallots and sweat for 5 minutes, then sprinkle with the sugar and cook gently for a further 10–15 minutes until golden brown and caramelised. Stir though the butter. Transfer to a blender and blitz until smooth. If too thick, thin with a little hot cream. Season with salt and pepper to taste. Transfer to a bowl and set aside.

For the couscous, using a microplane or swivel vegetable peeler, shave 200g Romanesco into a bowl; it should resemble couscous grains. Shave 150g cauliflower into a separate bowl. Bring the water to the boil in a medium saucepan. Add the shaved cauliflower and cook for 30 seconds, then add the shaved Romanesco and cook together for 30 seconds to 1 minute. Take off the heat, add the couscous and cover the pan tightly with cling film. Set aside for about 7 minutes until the couscous has absorbed all the water and is tender.

Meanwhile, heat the oven to 180°C/Gas 4. Season the guinea fowl breasts on both sides with salt and pepper. Roll each one into a sausage, wrap tightly in all-purpose cling film and twist and tie the ends to secure. Bring a large pan of salted water to a gentle simmer. Add the guinea fowl and poach for 7 minutes, then lift out and set aside to rest for 5 minutes.

Heat a drizzle of olive oil in a pan, add the chopped shallots and cook for 30 seconds. Add the sugar and wine vinegar and let the shallots caramelise lightly. Pour in the stock, bring to the boil and reduce by about half to a sauce consistency. Whisk in half of the salted butter.

Heat a non-stick ovenproof pan over a medium-high heat and add a drizzle of olive oil. Unwrap the guinea fowl breasts and season lightly. Place in the hot pan and colour all around, turning as necessary. Add the rest of the salted butter, heat until foaming and spoon over the guinea fowl. Place in the oven for a minute or two to heat through.

To serve, reheat the shallot purée if necessary. Fluff up the Romanesco couscous with a fork, season and fork though the extra virgin olive oil. Spoon onto warmed plates. Cut the guinea bowl breasts in half on an angle and arrange on the plates. Drizzle a little of the sauce over them. Add spoonfuls of shallot purée to finish. Serve with the rest of the sauce.

You can poach the guinea fowl in advance and keep them wrapped, ready to be finished in the pan just before serving. The couscous may seem tedious when you are shaving the Romanesco and cauli, but trust me, the end result more than justifies the effort.

Duck breast with parsnip tatin

Serves 6

6 boneless duck breasts
  (with skin), about 220g
  each
1 tbsp olive oil
4 pinches of ground cumin
100g butter, in pieces
200ml port
300ml veal stock
  (see page 185)
1 tsp pink peppercorns,
  lightly crushed
Sea salt and freshly ground
  black pepper

Parsnip tatins
3 medium parsnips
60g butter
6 tbsp honey
1 sheet of ready-rolled puff
  pastry, about 35 x 25cm

Butternut squash purée
400g butternut squash
50g salted butter
2 tbsp crème fraîche

To serve
200g turnip greens (tops)
1 tbsp olive oil
Knob of butter

Wine suggestion:
A juicy Pinot Noir from
South Africa or Burgundy

Heat the oven to 190°C/Gas 5. For the tatins, peel the parsnips, cut in half widthways, then quarter lengthways and cut out the cores. Add to a pan of boiling salted water and parboil for 2 minutes; they should still be a bit firm when tested with a knife. Drain and cool in iced water; drain well.

In a small pan, melt the butter and honey together and bring to the boil. Pour evenly into 6 individual flan tins, about 7cm in diameter. Score the backs of the parsnips deeply with the tip of a small knife, being careful not to cut all the way through. Lay the parsnips scored side down in the flan tins, close together so they fill the tins. Roll out the puff pastry a little more and cut out 6 circles, about 9cm in diameter. Lay the pastry discs on top of the parsnips and gently tuck the edges down inside the rim of the flan tins. Bake for 12–15 minutes until the pastry is golden brown.

Meanwhile, for the purée, peel the squash and cut into large chunks. Cook in a pan of boiling salted water for 8–10 minutes until tender. Drain well and tip into a blender. Heat the butter in the pan until just nutty brown, then pour into the blender and blitz the squash to a purée. Add the crème fraîche and pulse to combine. Season with salt and pepper. Put into a pan.

Score the skin of the duck breasts and season with salt and pepper. Heat a large ovenproof pan over a medium-high heat and drizzle in the olive oil. Add the duck breasts, skin side down, and colour for 4–5 minutes, until golden. Turn and sear the flesh side briefly. Turn the duck breasts skin side down again and sprinkle with the cumin. Dot with half of the butter and place in the oven to finish cooking for 5 minutes. Transfer to a warm plate and set aside to rest in a warm place while you make the sauce. When the tatins are ready, remove them from the oven and set aside with the duck.

Add the port to the pan used to cook the duck, stirring to deglaze, then let bubble to reduce to a syrupy consistency. Add the veal stock and reduce again until thickened, then whisk in the remaining butter. Wilt the turnip greens briefly in a hot pan with the olive oil and knob of butter. Season with salt and pepper to taste. Reheat the squash purée.

To serve, spoon the butternut squash purée onto warmed plates and drag a spoon through decoratively. Unmould the tatins onto the plates and add the wilted greens. Slice the duck breasts and arrange on the plates, sprinkle with pink peppercorns and serve with the sauce.

I love duck and *tartes tatins*, so pairing them is a great treat for me. You can make one large tatin to serve at the table rather than individual ones if you prefer. If you can't get hold of turnip greens, use spinach instead, doubling the quantity.

Lamb with figs, lemons and quinoa

Serves 6

6 lamb cannon portions
  (eye of loin), about
  180g each
Olive oil for cooking
50g salted butter
Sea salt and freshly ground
  black pepper

Herb and spice mix
1 tbsp marjoram leaves
3 tsp ras el hanout
2 tsp sea salt
6 white peppercorns

Figs and lemons
2 red onions, peeled
  and chopped
2 carrots, peeled and
  chopped
150ml Madeira
400ml brown chicken stock
  (see page 184) or veal
  stock (see page 185)
50g salted butter, in pieces
12 ready-to-eat figs, halved
6 preserved lemons, cut
  into small chunks
2 tbsp pine nuts, toasted

Quinoa
200g quinoa
600ml water
2 pinches of saffron strands
2 tbsp extra virgin olive oil
2 tbsp raisins

Wine suggestion:
A Sangiovese from Italy

For the herb and spice mix, using a pestle and mortar, crush the marjoram leaves, ras el hanout, salt and peppercorns; set aside. (Or chop the herbs, then crush the spices with the side of a large knife and combine.) Heat the oven to 180°C/Gas 4.

To make the sauce for the figs and lemons, heat a drizzle of olive oil in a medium saucepan over a medium heat. Add the onions and carrots and sweat for about 5 minutes until golden. Pour in the Madeira and let bubble to reduce by half. Pour in the stock and bring to the boil, then reduce down for about 20 minutes.

Meanwhile, to cook the quinoa, place in a saucepan with the water and saffron. Bring to the boil, then lower the heat to medium-low, cover with a lid and cook until tender, about 20 minutes.

While the quinoa is cooking, heat a non-stick ovenproof pan over a medium-high heat and add a drizzle of olive oil. Season the lamb with salt and pepper and add to the pan. Colour all over, turning as necessary until evenly golden brown. Add the butter and heat until foaming, then place in the oven to finish cooking. Allow 7 minutes for pink lamb, turning the meat halfway through cooking. Sprinkle with the herb and spice mix and set aside to rest in a warm place for 5 minutes.

Whisk the butter into the sauce, a piece at a time. Add the figs, chunks of preserved lemon and pine nuts, then correct the seasoning with salt and pepper. When the quinoa is ready, fluff it with a fork, season and fork through the extra virgin olive oil and raisins.

To serve, pile the quinoa into warmed deep plates or bowls and spoon the figs, lemons and sauce alongside. Cut each lamb cannon into 2 or 3 slices and place in the middle.

Quinoa, pronounced 'keen-wa', is often mistaken for a grain. It is, in fact, a highly nutritious seed – grown high in the Andes mountains of South America.

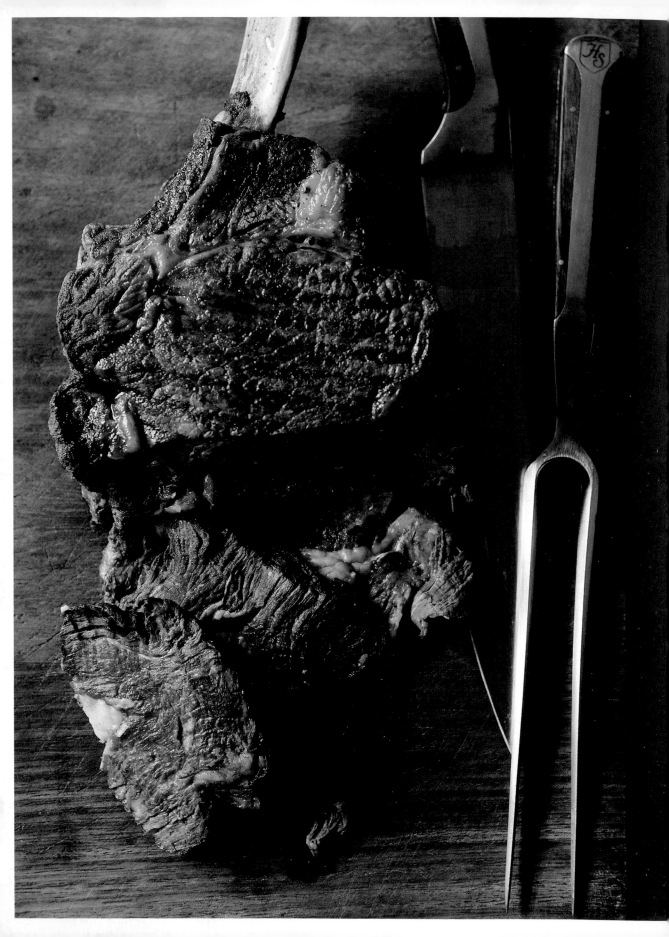

Rib of beef with potato puffs

Serves 4

1 large rib of beef, about 900g
Oil for drizzling
Sea salt and freshly ground back pepper

Hollandaise sauce
1 shallot, peeled and finely chopped
1 tsp white peppercorns, crushed
1 tbsp white wine vinegar
50ml water
3 medium egg yolks
200g warm clarified butter
Juice of ½ lemon, or to taste

Potato puffs
4 large potatoes (good chipping variety, such as Maris Piper)
3 medium egg whites
2 tbsp cornflour
600ml vegetable oil for deep-frying

Sautéed spinach
500g spinach leaves, washed
2 tbsp olive oil
1 tbsp butter (optional)
1 tsp finely chopped garlic

Wine suggestion:
A smooth Cabernet Sauvignon Merlot blend, from either Bordeaux or South Africa

Preheat the oven to 190°C/Gas 5. To make the hollandaise, put the shallot, crushed peppercorns, wine vinegar and water into a small saucepan and simmer gently until the shallot is translucent. Leave to cool, then whisk in the egg yolks over a very gentle heat or in a bain-marie. When the sauce is very thick, take off the heat and gently whisk in the clarified butter. Correct the seasoning with the lemon juice and salt. Keep warm over a bain-marie.

For the potato puffs, peel the potatoes and finely slice into rounds, about 1mm thin. Lay the slices out on kitchen paper. Using a pastry brush, brush half of the slices with egg white. Dip one side only of the remaining potato slices in the cornflour. Sandwich the potato slices together in pairs, egg-white coated side and cornflour-dipped sides together. Using a 2–3cm cutter, cut out discs from these.

Place an oven tray in the oven to heat up. Heat a griddle pan. Season the rib of beef with salt and pepper and drizzle with a little oil. Lay on the hot griddle pan until well browned, then turn and sear the other side. Transfer to the tray in the oven to finish cooking for about 30 minutes, turning halfway.

Meanwhile, heat the oil in a deep, heavy saucepan to about 180°C. Deep-fry the potato discs in batches as necessary until golden brown; they will puff up and form small balls. Remove and drain on kitchen paper. Season with salt and keep warm while you cook the rest.

When the rib of beef is cooked, rest in a warm place for 5 minutes. Just before serving, sauté the spinach in a large pan with the olive oil, butter if using, garlic and some salt and pepper, until just wilted.

Carve the beef and serve with the hollandaise sauce, sautéed spinach and potato puffs.

This one never fails to impress. Good-quality beef on the bone is succulent and flavoursome, the hollandaise sauce lends an elegant, luxurious touch and the potato puffs are a fun element.

Roast venison *with chocolate sauce*

Serves 6

6 portions of venison
  tenderloin, about 180g each
Olive oil for cooking
60g salted butter, in pieces
30g dark chocolate (70%
  cocoa solids), chopped
100ml port
50ml red wine
400ml veal stock
  (see page 185)
Sea salt and freshly ground
  black pepper

Braised red cabbage

1 small red cabbage, about
  700g
Olive oil for cooking
70g caster sugar
2 pinches of ground
  cinnamon
2 pinches of freshly grated
  nutmeg
2 pinches of ground cloves
2 pinches of ground allspice
120ml red wine vinegar
300ml port

Glazed chestnuts

50g salted butter
240g cooked peeled
  chestnuts (vacuum-packed
  are fine)
2 tbsp thin honey
100ml veal stock
  (see page 185)

To serve
Mash (see page 85)

Wine suggestion:
A deep Malbec from
Argentina

First prepare the braised cabbage. Quarter, core and thinly slice the red cabbage. Heat a wide flameproof casserole over a medium-high heat and add a good drizzle of olive oil. Add the cabbage and sweat for 5 minutes without colouring. Scatter over the sugar and cook for a further 5 minutes, then sprinkle in the spices and cook for 2 minutes. Add the wine vinegar and bring to the boil, then pour in the port. Cover the surface with a piece of greaseproof paper and cook over a gentle heat until the cabbage is tender and most of the liquid has reduced away, about 25 minutes.

Meanwhile, heat the oven to 180°C/Gas 4. For the glazed chestnuts, heat a non-stick frying pan over a medium-high heat, then add the butter followed by the chestnuts and honey. Cook, turning the chestnuts, until the honey caramelises, then pour in the veal stock, stirring. Let bubble to reduce over a medium heat for about 5 minutes until the liquor has reduced down to a glaze and coats the chestnuts. Keep warm.

Season the venison with salt and pepper. Heat a non-stick ovenproof pan over a medium-high heat, then add a drizzle of olive oil. Place the venison in the pan and colour all over, turning as necessary, until well browned on all sides. Add a knob or two of the butter and transfer to the oven to finish cooking. Allow 5 minutes for pink venison, turning halfway through cooking. Transfer the venison to a warm plate and set aside to rest in a warm place for 5 minutes.

For the sauce, put the chocolate into a bowl and set aside. Add the port and red wine to the pan used to cook the venison, stirring to deglaze, and let bubble to reduce by half. Pour in the veal stock and reduce again by half. Whisk in the rest of the butter and, just before serving, whisk into the chocolate to make a smooth sauce.

Spoon the creamy mash onto warmed plates and drag a spoon though decoratively. Pile the braised cabbage onto the plates. Slice the venison and arrange on top. Finish with the glazed chestnuts.

Here I've matched venison with a spiced red cabbage recipe I discovered while working in Holland with my friend Gerdy, who is a fabulous chef in her own right. With her front-of-house husband Jouk, she introduced me to my first European Michelin meals.

Coconut pannacotta *with mango jelly*

Serves 8

Mango jelly
2 sheets of leaf gelatine,
  2g each
300g mango purée
20g caster sugar
100ml water

Pannacotta
4½ sheets of leaf gelatine,
  2g each
600ml coconut milk
150ml double cream
240g caster sugar
100ml Malibu

Mango and lime salad
60g tapioca
60g mango purée
juice of 1 lime
100g caster sugar
100ml water
1 green mango
1 finger lime, halved, or
  ½ pink grapefruit

Coconut biscuits
120g plain flour
6g baking powder
110g caster sugar
110g butter, softened
1 medium egg
110g freshly grated coconut

Wine suggestion:
A sweet Muscat from France,
such as Beaumes de Venise,
or from South Africa

First make the biscuits. Sift the flour and baking powder into a bowl, stir in the sugar and rub in the butter until the mixture resembles crumbs. Incorporate the egg and grated coconut until evenly combined. Shape into a log, wrap in greaseproof paper and refrigerate for at least an hour.

Heat the oven to 180°C/Gas 4. Slice the biscuit dough into rounds, about 5mm thick, and place on a baking sheet lined with greaseproof paper. Bake for about 10 minutes until golden brown. Leave on the tray for a minute or two, then transfer to a wire rack to cool.

To make the jelly, soak the gelatine leaves in just enough cold water to cover for about 5 minutes to soften. Put the mango purée, sugar and water into a saucepan over a medium heat and bring just to the boil, then take off the heat. Drain the gelatine, squeeze out excess water, then add to the purée and stir until melted. Divide between 8 glass serving bowls and place in the fridge for about 15 minutes to set.

For the pannacotta, soak the gelatine in cold water to soften (as above). Put the rest of the ingredients in a saucepan and bring just to the boil, then take off the heat. Drain the gelatine, squeeze out excess water and then whisk into the pannacotta mixture until melted. Stand the bowl over a larger bowl of iced water and whisk until almost set but still pourable. Pour on top of the mango in the glasses and return to the fridge.

For the mango and lime salad, cook the tapioca in boiling water to cover by about 1cm for 10 minutes or until translucent. Drain and refresh in cold water; drain well. Stir half of the tapioca into the mango purée and mix the other half with the lime juice. Refrigerate until ready to serve. Dissolve the sugar in the water in a small pan over a medium heat, then bring to the boil to make a sugar syrup; leave to cool.

To serve, peel the green mango and cut the flesh into very fine dice, roughly the size of the tapioca pearls. Gently mix the tapiocas and diced green mango with a little of the sugar syrup to taste, then spoon on top of the set pannacottas. Scoop out the pink pearls from the finger lime or grapefruit and sprinkle over the salad. Serve with the coconut biscuits.

This dessert has come a long way since the early bouncy version I made in New Zealand just a few years into my cooking career. This refined recipe is soft, light and delicate. You can bake the biscuits a day ahead and keep them in an airtight tin.

Millefeuille of chilli chocolate and raspberries

Serves 6

3 filo pastry sheets
70g butter, melted and
  heated until nutty brown
50g icing sugar

Chocolate mousse filling
240g good-quality dark
  chocolate (70% cocoa
  solids), in pieces
50g caster sugar
50ml water
2 medium egg yolks
350ml whipping cream
2 tsp chilli powder

Caramel sauce
100g caster sugar
200ml double cream
1 tbsp salted butter

To assemble
230g raspberries, halved
  lengthways if large
15g pink pralines (see note,
  page 56), lightly crushed
15g pistachio nuts
  (unsalted), lightly crushed
6 scoops of pistachio ice
  cream (see page 187)
Icing sugar for dusting
Pinch of chilli powder

For the mousse filling, melt the chocolate in a bowl over a pan of gently simmering water, then take off the heat and let cool slightly. Dissolve the sugar in the water in a small pan over a medium heat, bring to the boil and let boil for 1 minute. Meanwhile, whisk the egg yolks in a large bowl and then gently pour in the boiled sugar syrup in a thin stream, whisking continuously as you do so. Continue whisking for 3–4 minutes or until thick and mousse-like. Carefully fold into the melted chocolate.

In another bowl, whisk the cream with the chilli powder to soft peaks and then gently fold through the chocolate mixture. Cover and place in the fridge for about 5 minutes to firm up.

Heat the oven to 180°C/Gas 4. Lay one sheet of filo on your work surface and brush with butter, then sift over a dusting of icing sugar. Lay another filo sheet on top and pat down firmly with your hands, then brush with butter and dust with icing sugar as before. Repeat with the third layer of filo. Using a large sharp knife, cut the pastry neatly in half lengthways and then cut each piece across into about 12 strips. (You need 3 strips per portion, but you may need extra in case of breakages.)

Line a baking sheet with baking parchment. Place the sandwiched filo strips on the tray, cover with another sheet of baking parchment and place another baking tray on top. Put a heavy weight, such as a casserole dish, on top to keep it flat. Bake for 12–15 minutes, until golden brown. Leave the filo to cool with the tray on top or the strips will curl up.

To make the caramel sauce, melt the sugar in a small saucepan over a medium heat and continue to heat until it starts to caramelise at the edges. Now stir with a spatula until all the sugar has caramelised. Remove from the heat and whisk in the cream, taking care as it can bubble up rapidly. Stir in the butter and set aside to cool.

(continued overleaf)

Wine suggestion:
A young Tawny Port
(10 years old)

I first came across the combination of chilli and chocolate while living and working in Mauritius. Come to think of it, most of what we ate there had chilli in it, so much so that at one point I could eat raw chillies like the Mauritians – dipped in salt along with a lamb curry. Those days are long gone, but this combination will always remind me of Mauritius.

To assemble, put the mousse into a piping bag fitted with a large plain nozzle (or you can simply scoop it if you prefer). Put a small dot of the mousse on each large serving plate and lay a strip of filo pastry on top (the mousse will stop it slipping on the plate).

Pipe a thick line of mousse along one side of the pastry. Place a line of raspberries along the middle of the pastry, then pipe another line of mousse on the other side. Place another strip of filo on top and press down lightly, then repeat the mousse and raspberry layer. Position a third piece of filo on top of the mousse and berries, pressing it down lightly.

Drizzle the caramel sauce decoratively onto the plates and sprinkle with some of the crushed pralines and pistachios. Place a scoop of pistachio ice cream on top and sprinkle with pistachios. Dust the tops of the pastries with icing sugar and a little chilli powder and serve at once.

Floating on chocolate

Serves 6–8

Chocolate crème anglaise
400ml milk
100ml double cream
6 medium egg yolks
65g caster sugar
100g good-quality dark
chocolate (70% cocoa
solids), in small pieces

Caramel
150g caster sugar

Poaching syrup
4 tbsp caster sugar
1 litre water

Meringue
200ml egg whites
(6–7 medium)
Finely grated zest of 1 lemon
(ideally a bergamot lemon)
70g caster sugar
2 tsp lemon juice

To serve
50g chocolate pearls
(or similar)

Wine suggestion:
A fortified sweet wine from
Banyuls, France

To make the chocolate anglaise, pour the milk and cream into a heavy-based saucepan and slowly bring to the boil. Meanwhile, whisk the egg yolks and sugar together in a bowl, then pour on the hot creamy milk, whisking as you do so. Return the mixture to the saucepan and cook, stirring, over a medium-low heat until the custard is thick enough to coat the back of the wooden spoon (at 82°C); do not allow to boil.

Put the chocolate pieces into a large bowl and pour on the hot custard, whisking as you do so. Continue to whisk until all the chocolate is melted and the custard is smooth. Set aside to cool to room temperature.

For the caramel, melt the sugar in a wide heavy-based pan and cook to a golden caramel, then remove from the heat and leave to cool slightly.

For the poaching syrup, dissolve the sugar in the water in a wide pan and bring to a gentle simmer. Meanwhile, to make the meringues, whisk the egg whites in a clean bowl to stiff peaks and add the lemon zest. Gradually whisk in the sugar, 1 tbsp at a time, then whisk in the lemon juice.

Either scoop the meringue into 6–8 ovals and drop into the poaching syrup or use a metal ring to shape into neat rounds and drop it into the syrup – the meringue will puff up and you can remove the ring. Poach for about 1 minute, gently ladling a little of the poaching syrup over the meringues as they cook. Lift out the cooked meringues with a slotted spoon and place on a wire rack to drain.

Using a fork, drizzle the warm caramel decoratively over the meringues (you might like to practise this first on greaseproof paper). Leave to set for 1 minute, then gently tap around the base to break off the excess caramel.

To serve, scatter the chocolate pearls in shallow serving bowls, pour on the chocolate sauce, then float the meringues on top. Serve at once.

Floating islands, or *oeufs à la neige* as it is known in France, is one of the first things I ever made at Le Gavroche. This is my version of the great classic, with a dark chocolate crème anglaise for pure indulgence.

Pear soufflé with salted caramel sauce

Serves 4–6

1 tbsp softened butter,
  to grease the dishes
400ml water
220g caster sugar
4 firm, ripe pears
1½ tbsp cornflour
260ml egg whites
  (about 8 medium)
Knob of butter

Salted caramel sauce

200g caster sugar
400ml cream
60g salted butter, softened

Wine suggestion:
A chilled Moscato d'Asti

Butter 4–6 ramekins or ovenproof dishes, about 7cm wide and 4cm deep, with the soft butter, and chill in the fridge.

Put the water and 100g sugar into a saucepan that will hold the pears and dissolve over a low heat. Meanwhile, core and peel the pears. Add to the sugar syrup and poach until tender – up to 20 minutes, depending on ripeness; test with the point of a knife. Leave to cool in the liquid.

Take out 2 pears and purée in a blender, then place in another saucepan. Dissolve the cornflour in 2 tbsp of the cooled poaching liquor. Add to the pear purée and bring to the boil, stirring. Cook, stirring, to thicken the purée. Transfer to a bowl and cover with cling film. Take out the other 2 pears, cut into 1cm cubes, cover with cling film and set aside for serving.

To make the salted caramel sauce, scatter the sugar evenly in a heavy-based pan and melt over a medium heat, then cook to a dark caramel, stirring with a wooden spoon to encourage it to cook evenly. Take off the heat and stir in the cream, taking care as the hot caramel may splutter. Stir until smooth, then whisk in the salted butter and set aside.

Preheat the oven to 180°C/Gas 4. Whisk the egg whites, using an electric whisk on a medium speed, until they form stiff peaks. Gradually add the remaining 120g sugar, a spoonful at a time, whisking constantly until it is all incorporated and you have a thick, shiny meringue.

In a separate bowl, whisk the pear purée to a smooth paste. Whisk in a large spoonful of the meringue to loosen it, then carefully fold in the remaining meringue, with a large metal spoon, until evenly incorporated.

Spoon the mixture into the prepared dishes and lightly tap them on the work surface to remove air pockets. Gently level the tops with the edge of a spatula, wipe the edge of the dishes clean and place on an oven tray.

Bake in the oven until the soufflés are well risen and holding their shape, 6–8 minutes, depending on the size of the dishes. Meanwhile, lightly pan-fry the pear cubes in a little butter and keep warm. As you take the soufflés from the oven, insert a spoonful of diced pears through the top of each one and pour in the salted caramel. Serve at once.

So many people have a fear of making soufflés, believing it to be much more difficult than it actually is. Perhaps it should be a well-kept secret, but I enjoy teaching friends how easy they are!

Praline macaroons with caramelised apples

Serves 6–7

Macaroons
220g icing sugar
130g ground almonds
100g caster sugar
2 tbsp water
130ml egg whites
  (about 4 medium)

Praline mousse
125g salted butter, softened
2 medium eggs, separated
75g hazelnut praline paste
  (see below)
125g caster sugar
2 tbsp water

Caramelised apples
3 Braeburn or Granny Smith
  apples
4 tbsp caster sugar
2 tbsp salted butter
3 tbsp cider vinegar

To serve
70g good-quality milk
  chocolate, in pieces
Salted caramel sauce
  (see page 148)
2 tbsp crushed hazelnuts
  to sprinkle

Wine suggestion:
A classic Sauternes

For the macaroons, heat the oven to 140°C/Gas 1. Sift the icing sugar and ground almonds together, pressing through the sieve if necessary; set aside. Dissolve the sugar in the water in a small pan, then bring to the boil and let boil for 2 minutes. Meanwhile, whisk the egg whites in a clean bowl to stiff peaks, then gently pour in the boiled sugar syrup in a thin steam, whisking continuously as you do so. Fold in the almond and icing sugar mixture in 3 stages until evenly combined; do not overmix or the mixture will become too runny.

Put the mixture into a piping bag fitted with a 1cm plain nozzle. Line a large baking sheet with baking parchment and draw on 12–14 circles, 5cm in diameter, then invert the paper. Pipe the mixture onto the circles to cover them evenly. Bake for 20 minutes, then leave to cool on the tray. Gently lift off the macaroons with a palette knife onto a wire rack.

For the mousse, whisk the butter, egg yolks and praline paste together in a bowl until smooth; set aside. Dissolve the sugar in the water in a small saucepan, bring to the boil and let boil for 2 minutes. Meanwhile, whisk the egg whites in a clean bowl to stiff peaks, then whisk in the boiled sugar syrup in a thin steam. Whisk this meringue until cool, then fold into the praline mixture. Cover and chill in the fridge.

For the caramelised apples, heat the oven to 180°C/Gas 4. Peel the apples and cut into thick batons. Put the sugar into a large non-stick ovenproof pan over a medium-high heat and let it melt and caramelise slightly. Add the apples and toss to coat in the caramel. Add the butter and toss the apples gently. Add the cider vinegar and let bubble for 30 seconds. Transfer the pan to the oven and cook for 5 minutes. Keep warm.

To assemble, melt the chocolate in a bowl over a pan of gently simmering water, then whisk into the caramel sauce. Spoon some praline mousse onto the flat side of half of the macaroons and sandwich together in pairs with the rest. Place a dollop of praline mousse on each plate and top with the macaroons or serve them all on a platter. Drizzle over some of the sauce, add the caramelised apples and finish with the crushed hazelnuts.

These look great served all together on a platter. If you cannot find hazelnut praline paste, prepare your own. Make a light caramel with 200g caster sugar, 50g liquid glucose and 50ml water. Add 125g each of toasted, skinned almonds and hazelnuts, then pour onto a tray and leave to harden. Break up the praline and blitz to a powder in a blender, in 3 or 4 batches. Keep in a sealed jar.

Rhubarb cake with crumble ice cream

Serves 6

Rhubarb layer

25g butter, softened
4 sticks of rhubarb (ideally
    forced), about 300g
100g caster sugar

Cake mixture

80g plain flour
1 tsp baking powder
20g ground almonds
2 tsp ground ginger
1 medium egg
2 tbsp crème fraîche
1 tbsp vegetable oil
60g caster sugar

Crumble ice cream

1.5 litres crème anglaise
    (see page 186)
80g oats
45g demerara sugar
45g plain flour
80g butter, in pieces

Rhubarb crisps

Rhubarb trimmings
    (from above)
150g sugar
150ml water

Wine suggestion:
A rosé Champagne or
sparkling rosé

First make the crumble ice cream. Heat the oven to 180°C/Gas 4. Chill the crème anglaise. Put the oats, sugar, flour and butter into a bowl and rub together with your fingertips to make a crumble, then scatter on a baking tray and bake for about 10 minutes until golden. Tip onto a tray and leave to cool, then break up the crumble with your fingers. Churn the crème anglaise in an ice-cream maker until thick, about 20 minutes. Fold the crumble mix through the ice cream and freeze in a suitable container.

Spread the softened butter over the bottom of a loaf tin, about 30 x 7cm. Wash the rhubarb and pat dry. Cut 7cm batons (the width of the tin) and toss in the sugar; reserve the rhubarb trimmings. Sprinkle some of the sugar from the rhubarb evenly over the butter in the tin. Lay the rhubarb batons side by side in the tin to cover the base and sprinkle with more of the sugar. Add another layer of rhubarb and more sugar. Set aside.

For the rhubarb crisps, heat the oven to 160°C/Gas 3. Using a mandoline or swivel vegetable peeler, cut 8–10 fine slices from the rhubarb trimmings. Dissolve the sugar in the water in a small pan over a medium heat, bring to the boil and boil for 1 minute, then set aside to cool. Drop the rhubarb slices into the cooled syrup, then lift the slices onto a baking tray lined with baking parchment. Cover with another sheet of parchment and place another flat tray on top. Bake for 8–10 minutes until crisp. Leave to cool, then scrape off the paper with a spatula or knife.

For the cake, heat the oven to 180°C/Gas 4. Mix the flour, baking powder, ground almonds and ginger together in a large bowl. In another bowl, whisk together the egg, crème fraîche, oil and caster sugar, then whisk into the flour mixture.

Either put the cake mixture into a piping bag fitted with a large nozzle and gently pipe along the top of the rhubarb to cover, or simply spread it over with the back of a spoon or a spatula. Bake for 25 minutes until golden and springy to the touch. Leave to rest in the tin for 5 minutes before inverting onto a plate.

Slice the rhubarb cake and serve warm with a scoop of crumble ice cream, topped with a rhubarb crisp.

This is a delight to serve. The juices from the rhubarb and sugar soak through the cake – making it deliciously moist. You may think there isn't enough cake mixture, but you will find it rises considerably in the oven.

Gianduja choux buns

Serves 6

Choux paste
65ml water
60ml milk
Pinch of fine sea salt
50g butter
75g plain flour
2 medium eggs
1 egg yolk, beaten, for
   eggwash

Gianduja chocolate filling
200g Gianduja milk
   chocolate, in pieces
60g caster sugar
120ml single cream
1 large egg yolk
300ml double cream

Caramel topping
200g caster sugar

Wine suggestion:
A Pedro Ximénez sweet sherry

Heat the oven to 200°C/Gas 6. To make the choux paste, put the water, milk, salt and butter into a medium saucepan and bring to the boil. Add the flour all at once and stir vigorously with a spatula to combine. Continue to stir over a medium-low heat for about 5 minutes until the mixture forms a ball and leaves the side of the pan clean, then remove from the heat and allow to cool slightly for a few minutes.

Beat the eggs into the mixture, one at a time, to make a smooth, shiny choux paste. Put the mixture into a piping bag fitted with a large plain nozzle. Line a large baking sheet with greaseproof paper. Pipe 12–14 large choux mounds in rows onto the paper.

Brush the choux buns with egg wash and bake for 10 minutes. Lower the oven setting to 180°C/Gas 4 and bake for a further 20 minutes. Transfer the buns to a wire rack and leave to cool.

To make the filling, melt the chocolate in a bowl over a pan of gently simmering water, then take off the heat and set aside. Tip the sugar into a small saucepan and place over a medium heat to melt. Continue to cook to a golden caramel, then take off the heat and whisk in the single cream.

Put the egg yolk into a large bowl and whisk in the caramel cream mixture. Pour this mixture onto the melted chocolate and fold together. Allow to cool slightly. Finally, whip the double cream to soft peaks and fold into the mixture.

For the caramel topping, melt the sugar in a wide pan over a medium heat and cook to a golden caramel, then remove from the heat. Dip the choux buns into the caramel to coat the tops; allow to set. Cut the choux buns in half and pipe the cream into the bases to fill generously. Replace the lids. Serve the buns on a large plate.

I like to make these as large as possible because I don't know anyone that doesn't like choux buns. And I fill them generously with the creamy milk chocolate filling. The recipe makes enough for two per person.

Something Different

Coronation chicken soup

Serves 6 as a starter

1kg chicken drumsticks
Olive oil for brushing and
  cooking
2 pinches of white
  peppercorns
1 onion, peeled and roughly
  chopped
2 celery sticks, de-stringed
  with a peeler and roughly
  chopped
1 leek (white part only),
  washed and roughly
  chopped
2 litres water
100ml double cream
  (optional)
Sea salt and freshly ground
  black pepper

Curried mayonnaise

1 tbsp mild curry powder
2 tbsp mayonnaise
120ml whipping cream,
  whipped

Watercress oil

30g watercress,
  trimmed
120ml rapeseed oil

To finish

6 ready-to-eat dried
  apricots, thinly sliced
Few watercress sprigs,
  leaves only

Heat the oven to 180°C/Gas 4. Line a baking tray with baking parchment. Carefully remove the skins from 6 chicken drumsticks, trying to avoid tearing them. Cut them in half, so you have two complete circles from each. Wrap 6 metal dowels with baking parchment, twisting the ends to secure. Brush lightly with oil, then gently thread the chicken skins on. Place on the baking tray and bake until golden, about 12 minutes. Leave to rest for 2 minutes, then remove while still warm. If you find they have stuck, slice through with a sharp knife and carefully peel off

Heat a medium saucepan over a medium-high heat and add a drizzle of olive oil. Add the drumsticks, 2 pinches of salt and the peppercorns. Colour the chicken, turning as necessary, for about 4 minutes until golden. Add the onion, celery and leek, lower the heat and cook gently for 2–3 minutes to soften. Pour in the water and bring to the boil. Lower the heat and simmer gently for about 1 hour until the chicken is tender.

Meanwhile, for the curried mayonnaise, whisk the curry powder into the mayonnaise until evenly blended, then fold in the whipped cream and season with salt and pepper to taste.

For the watercress oil, blitz the watercress with the rapeseed oil in a blender to a purée.

Once the drumsticks are cooked, lift them out onto a board. Strain the soup through a sieve into a blender. Strip the chicken from the bones, discarding the rest of the skin. Reserve 4 heaped tbsp meat for serving. Add the rest to the soup in the blender and blitz until smooth. Return to the pan, add the cream, if using, and bring to a simmer. Correct the seasoning.

To serve, reheat the shredded chicken meat in a little of the soup. Place a little in each bowl with the sliced apricots. Carefully pour the soup around, then place a spoonful of curried mayonnaise on top of the chicken and apricot mix. Trickle the watercress oil around the soup. Finish with the golden chicken skin crowns and a few watercress leaves.

This soup is inspired by the original Coronation chicken salad created for the Queen's coronation. It is my dish to celebrate Her Majesty's Diamond Jubilee.

Sweetcorn soup with popcorn

Serves 6 as a starter

6 corn-on-the-cobs, or
  1kg frozen sweetcorn
  kernels, thawed
Olive oil for cooking
2 onions, peeled and thinly
  sliced
1.2 litres chicken stock
  (see page 184)
150ml single cream
  (optional)
20g popcorn
Knob of salted butter
6 slices of good-quality
  Parma ham
Sea salt and freshly ground
  black pepper

If using fresh corn, cut the kernels from the cobs, using a sharp knife; you need 1kg kernels. Heat a medium saucepan over a medium heat and add a drizzle of olive oil. Add the onions and sweat for about 5 minutes to soften without colouring. Add the corn kernels and cook for a further 2 minutes. Pour in the stock and bring to the boil. Turn down the heat to a gentle simmer and cook for 15 minutes.

Scoop out 2 heaped tbsp of the cooked corn kernels into a bowl and reserve for the garnish. Tip the soup into a blender and blitz until smooth, then return to the saucepan. Whisk in the cream, if using, and season with salt and pepper to taste.

In a small saucepan over a medium-high heat, heat 1 tbsp olive oil. Add the popcorn, put the lid on and shake the pan occasionally until all the corn has popped. Remove from the heat and add the knob of butter.

Spoon the popcorn and reserved corn into warm soup bowls and add a slice of Parma ham to each. Pour on the hot soup at the table.

This original soup with its popcorn garnish adds a fun element to dinner, especially if there are children around the table. It also works wonderfully with a few pieces of smoked chicken instead of the Parma ham.

Goat's milk pannacotta with pine nut crumble

Serves 6 as a starter

7 sheets of leaf gelatine,
  2g each
750ml goat's milk
250ml single cream
2 sage sprigs
10 cardamom pods
2 tsp fine salt

Crumble

200g plain flour
150g cold salted butter,
  diced
50g pistachio nuts
  (unsalted), skinned
100g pine nuts

To finish

Sunflower oil for
  brushing
6 sage leaves

To make the pannacotta, soak the gelatine leaves in enough cold water to cover for about 5 minutes to soften. Put the goat's milk, single cream, sage sprigs, cardamom pods and salt into a large saucepan. Place over a medium-low heat and slowly bring to the boil. Take off the heat. Drain the gelatine, squeeze out excess water and add to the pannacotta mixture, stirring until completely melted.

Strain the pannacotta mixture through a fine sieve into a jug, then pour into 6 ramekins or small dishes. Refrigerate for about 3 hours until set.

For the crumble, heat the oven to 180°C/Gas 4 and line a baking tray with greaseproof paper. Put the flour into a bowl and rub in the butter with your fingertips until the mixture is crumbly. Roughly crush the pistachios and pine nuts with a rolling pin and mix into the crumble. Place on the prepared tray and bake in the oven for about 7 minutes. Tip the crumble onto a plate, leave to cool, then run through your fingers to break it up.

For the garnish, cover a flat plate with a piece of cling film, brush with a little oil and sprinkle with salt and pepper. Place the sage leaves on the cling film and brush them lightly with oil. Cover with another piece of cling film and microwave on high until crispy, about 2 minutes; set aside.

Remove the pannacottas from the fridge 5–10 minutes before serving. Spoon a generous mound of crumble on top of each one and finish with a crispy sage leaf.

This goat's milk pannacotta with its contrasting crunchy topping is a lovely light starter – best served in small glass dishes or ramekins. Prepare the pannacottas ahead and refrigerate, but bring them to room temperature before serving.

Pacific Island style cured fish

Serves 6 as a starter

650g very fresh stone bass
  fillets
Finely grated zest and juice
  of 2 lemons
5 medium tomatoes
3 celery sticks, de-stringed
  with a peeler
3 spring onions, trimmed
400ml coconut milk
Sea salt
Lime leaves to garnish
  (optional)

Remove the skin from the stone bass fillets, trim if necessary and check for pin bones, removing any with kitchen tweezers. Dice the fish into small cubes, about 1cm, and place in a bowl. Season with 3 generous pinches of salt. Add the lemon zest and the juice of 1 lemon. Toss well, then cover and place in the fridge to cure for 10 minutes.

Meanwhile, immerse the tomatoes in a bowl of hot water for 30 seconds or so to loosen the skins, then drain and peel. Halve and deseed the tomatoes, then cut the flesh into 5mm dice. Cut the celery into similar-sized dice. Slice the spring onions thinly on the diagonal.

Fold the tomatoes, celery and spring onions through the cured fish, then fold in the coconut milk. Taste and adjust the seasoning with the remaining lemon juice and a pinch of salt as required. Leave to stand for 5 minutes before serving, garnished with lime leaves if available.

This is truly one of my earliest memories of Samoan cuisine, and to this day it is still one of my favourites. If you are unable to buy stone bass, opt for sea bass or bream instead. Freshness is the key.

Cured mackerel with pickled vegetables

Serves 4 as a starter

4 very fresh mackerel fillets
3 tbsp sea salt
300ml white wine vinegar
200ml water
80g caster sugar
2 tarragon sprigs
Sea salt and freshly ground
   black pepper

Cauliflower purée
250g cauliflower
150ml double cream

Pickled vegetables
2 radishes
1 small kohlrabi
2 cauliflower florets
1/2 cucumber

Salad garnish
30g mixed salad leaves
1 punnet of micro-cress
Few chives, snipped
Splash of olive oil

Check the mackerel fillets for pin bones, removing any with kitchen tweezers. Lay skin side down on a plastic tray and scatter liberally with the 3 tbsp sea salt. Cover with cling film and place in the fridge for 30 minutes. Dust off the salt and wipe the fillets with kitchen paper. Place back on the tray.

For the pickling liquor, put the wine vinegar, water, sugar and tarragon sprigs into a saucepan and slowly bring to the boil. Take off the heat and set aside to infuse for 2–3 minutes. Strain 200ml of the pickling liquor and reserve for the vegetables.

While still hot, but not boiling, pour the rest of the pickling liquor over the mackerel. Leave for a minute or two, then take out the mackerel and carefully peel away the skin. Place the mackerel back in the pickling liquor, cover and leave in the fridge for 30 minutes.

For the cauliflower purée, chop the cauliflower into small pieces and cook in boiling salted water for about 5 minutes until soft. Drain and return to the saucepan. Add the cream, bring to a simmer and season with salt and pepper. Transfer to a blender and blitz until very smooth. Spoon into a small bowl.

Reheat the reserved pickling liquor to simmering, then take off the heat and set aside. Thinly slice the radishes and kohlrabi, using a swivel vegetable peeler or mandoline. Cut the cauliflower into tiny florets. Use a melon baller to scoop the cucumber into little balls. Place all the vegetables in the warm liquor and leave to pickle for about 10 minutes. Drain and pat dry on kitchen paper before serving.

When ready to serve, toss the salad leaves and chives with a little olive oil and season with salt and pepper. Spread the cauliflower purée thinly on a serving platter or individual plates. Cut each mackerel fillet into 2 or 3 pieces and place on the purée. Arrange the pickled vegetables and salad around the mackerel and serve.

Curing mackerel in this way gives a delicious and very different way to enjoy this fabulous fish. The pickled vegetables help to cut through the richness of the oily flesh. It works well with very fresh salmon too.

Steamed pork and mushroom buns

**Serves 8 as a starter
  or snack**

Dough

30g fresh yeast
225ml tepid water
340g self-raising flour,
  plus extra for dusting
  and kneading

Filling

200g pork fillet
500ml chicken stock
  (see page 184)
1 tbsp olive oil
1 tbsp sesame oil
80g oyster mushrooms,
  shredded
60g cabbage, cored and
  finely sliced
15g fresh root ginger, peeled
  and chopped
1 tbsp soy sauce
1/4 red chilli or less, to taste,
  deseeded and finely diced
1 tsp cornflour, blended with
  1 tbsp water

To prepare the dough, crumble the yeast into the warm water in a jug and mix to a paste. Put the flour into a large bowl, make a well in the middle and add the yeast liquid. Mix with your hand to form a smooth dough that comes together in a ball and leaves the sides of the bowl clean. Cover the bowl with a damp cloth and set aside for 10 minutes.

Dust your work surface with flour and turn the dough onto it. Knead well for a minute or so. Place on a lightly floured tray, cover loosely with cling film and set aside in a warm place to prove for 30–40 minutes until doubled in size.

Cut the pork into bite-sized 1cm pieces. Boil the chicken stock in a pan until reduced to 150ml, then set aside. Heat the olive and sesame oils in a large non-stick wok or frying pan over a medium-high heat. Add the pork and colour for 2–3 minutes, stirring, until nicely browned.

Add the mushrooms to the pork and cook for 1 minute, then add the cabbage and cook for another minute. Add the ginger, toss for a minute, then add the soy sauce and chilli. Add the reduced stock and bring to the boil, then stir in the blended cornflour and cook, stirring, for 2–3 minutes. Tip the mixture into a tray, let cool, then chill in the fridge for an hour.

Knock back the dough on a floured surface, dust with extra flour and knead for 1 minute. Divide into 8 even pieces. Dust your hands with a little flour and press out each piece of dough with the palm of your hand to a round, about 5m thick. Place a generous spoonful of the pork mixture in the middle of each round. Fold up the edges and press together to seal, then cut or twist off the excess dough.

Bring the water in your steamer to the boil. Turn the buns join side down and place each one on a square of baking parchment in the steamer tray. Cover and steam for 10 minutes. Lift the buns out and leave them to rest for about 5 minutes. Serve while still warm.

Again, this is a recipe from my Samoan background. There is a huge Asian influence in our cuisine. Typically these buns are filled with a simple pork and soy mix, and normally there is more dough than filling. I've added a few more ingredients to the filling and used much less dough.

Dad's stewed octopus *my way*

Serves 8

1.5kg octopus, cleaned
1 lemon, cut in half
2 garlic cloves, peeled
2 bay leaves
3 lemon thyme sprigs

Pearl barley
1 tbsp olive oil
½ onion, peeled and
  finely chopped
200g pearl barley
650ml chicken stock
  (see page 184)
40g squid ink

Sauce
1 tbsp olive oil
½ onion, peeled and finely
  diced
2 tsp mild curry powder
2 tsp ground turmeric
100ml white wine
200ml coconut milk
150ml single cream
Freshly ground white pepper

Samphire
15g butter
80g samphire, picked
  and washed
Sea salt and freshly ground
  black pepper

To finish
Finely grated zest of 1 lime

Heat the oven to 180°C/Gas 4. Rinse the octopus and place in a casserole with the lemon, garlic, bay and lemon thyme. There is no need to add liquid as the octopus releases a lot during cooking. Do not add any salt. Put the lid on and cook in the oven until soft and tender, about 1¾ hours. Remove the lid and leave the octopus to cool in its liquid.

To cook the pearl barley, heat a saucepan over a medium-high heat and drizzle in the olive oil. Add the onion and sweat over a medium heat for 1 minute, then add the pearl barley and cook, stirring, for 1 minute. Add half of the chicken stock and simmer until it is all absorbed before adding the rest. Cook over a medium heat until the pearl barley grains swell and soften, yet remain firm to the bite, about 25 minutes; it should be moist but not too wet. Tip in the squid ink and stir to coat the grains in the ink.

Strain 400ml of the cooking liquor from the octopus to use for the sauce. Heat a saucepan over a medium-high heat and drizzle in the olive oil. Add the onion and sweat for 2 minutes, then add the spices and cook, stirring for 1 minute. Add the wine, stirring to deglaze, then pour in the 400ml reserved octopus liquor and bring to the boil. Simmer to reduce over a medium heat for about 10 minutes. Pour in the coconut milk and cream and continue to simmer for 5 minutes to make a vibrant sauce. Correct the seasoning with a pinch of salt and a few twists of white pepper.

To cook the samphire, melt the butter in a pan over a medium-high heat, add the samphire and cook, tossing the leaves, for 2 minutes. Season with salt and pepper to taste.

To serve, cut the octopus into bite-sized pieces and gently reheat in a little of its cooking juice or some of the sauce. Divide the pearl barley between warmed serving bowls and spoon the samphire on top. Arrange the octopus in the middle. Froth the sauce, using a handheld stick blender to make it foamy and spoon around the samphire. Sprinkle with lime zest to finish.

I remember the last time my father cooked octopus, though I was only 12 years old. Earlier in the day, we had been fishing together off the beach and his line got caught up. I waded out to release it to find an octopus on the end, which promptly wrapped itself around my leg. I came out screaming and my father fell to the ground laughing. For that reason, I feel I have every right to make his recipe mine!

Veal on glass noodles

4 portions of veal fillet,
  about 180g each
2 tbsp olive oil
4 thyme sprigs
3 rosemary sprigs
Knob of butter
2 shallots, peeled and
  finely chopped
2 garlic cloves, peeled and
  finely chopped
90ml dark soy sauce
350ml veal stock
  (see page 185)
50g unsalted butter, in
  pieces
Sea salt and freshly ground
  black pepper

Glass noodles

100g vermicelli noodles
500ml boiling water
1 tbsp rapeseed or
  vegetable oil
1 tbsp sesame oil
2 tbsp chopped chives

Cabbage

1 Hispi or Sweetheart
  cabbage, cored
40g unsalted butter
1/2 garlic clove, peeled and
  finely chopped

Heat the oven to 190°C/Gas 5. Season the veal with salt and pepper. Heat an ovenproof frying pan over a medium-high heat and add a drizzle of olive oil. Add the veal and colour on all sides, allowing about 2 minutes and turning as necessary. Transfer to the oven and cook for 7–8 minutes for pink veal.

When the veal is ready, line a roasting tray with foil and place the thyme and rosemary sprigs in the tray. Now scorch the herbs, using a cook's blowtorch or by placing under a hot grill. As soon as any flame has died down, lay the veal on the smoking herbs. Quickly cover with another piece of foil to keep the smoke in. Set aside; keep warm.

Add a knob of butter to the hot pan (used to cook the veal), then add the shallots and cook for 1 minute. Add the chopped garlic and cook for 10 seconds, then add the soy sauce and let bubble to reduce by half. Pour in the veal stock and bring to the boil. Lower the heat to medium and simmer to reduce for 15 minutes.

Meanwhile, for the noodles, put the vermicelli into a large bowl and pour on the boiling water. Cover the bowl with cling film and set aside to soften, about 5–8 minutes. Remove the cling film and use a pair of scissors to chop through the noodles while they are still in the water. Drain thoroughly, then return to the bowl and toss through the rapeseed and sesame oils, and the chives.

While the noodles are soaking, cut the cabbage into bite-sized pieces and cook in boiling salted water or in a steamer for a few minutes until just tender. Drain, then briefly toss in a non-stick pan over a medium-high heat with the butter and garlic. Season with salt and pepper to taste.

To finish the sauce, whisk in the butter off the heat, a piece at a time, to give it a shine.

To serve, place a portion of noodles in the middle of each warm serving bowl and top with the cabbage. Spoon the sauce around the noodles. Slice each portion of veal into 3 or 4 pieces and place on top of the cabbage.

This dish is my adaptation of a Samoan chop suey. It has the same basic ingredients of vermicelli, garlic and soy sauce, but I have used veal instead of beef strips and cooked the components my way.

Roast lamb with black garlic purée

Serves 4

4 portions of lamb racks,
  about 250g each
3 tbsp olive oil
Sea salt and freshly ground
  black pepper

Black garlic purée

2 black garlic bulbs, cloves
  separated and peeled
200ml chicken stock
  (see page 184)
Knob of butter

Vegetables

3 medium potatoes
  (ideally Roosters)
400ml olive oil
100g shelled broad beans
2 tomatoes (ideally an
  heirloom variety)
1 small preserved lemon
Knob of butter
100ml chicken stock
  (see page 184)

Sauce

100ml white wine
300ml brown chicken stock
  (see page 184)
60g salted butter, in pieces
1 tbsp chopped green olives
1 tbsp chopped tarragon
  leaves

To finish

Oil for brushing
20 tarragon leaves

To make the garlic purée, put the black cloves in a saucepan with the stock, bring to the boil and simmer for 2 minutes. Tip into a blender and blitz until smooth, then return to the pan and stir in the butter; set aside.

Peel the potatoes and cut 8 discs, each 4cm in diameter and 2cm thick. Heat a griddle pan over a high heat. Brush the potato discs with a little of the olive oil, season with salt and pepper, then place on the griddle to char decoratively. Meanwhile, heat the rest of the olive oil in a saucepan over a low heat. Place the char-griddled potatoes in the oil and cook very gently for 25 minutes until tender. Remove to a tray and set aside.

Blanch the broad beans in boiling salted water for 2 minutes, then drain and refresh in cold water. Drain and slip the beans out of their skins. Immerse the tomatoes in a bowl of boiling water for 30 seconds or so to loosen the skins, then drain and peel. Halve and deseed the tomatoes, then cut the flesh into 1cm cubes. Remove and reserve the skin from the preserved lemon. Cut the lemon flesh into small pieces. Finely chop the lemon skin. Set all aside.

Heat the oven to 190°C/Gas 5. Season the lamb with salt and pepper. Heat a non-stick ovenproof pan over a medium-high heat and drizzle in the olive oil. Add the lamb racks and colour well on all sides, turning as necessary. Transfer to the oven and cook for 10–12 minutes for pink lamb, turning halfway through cooking. Remove to a warm platter; keep warm.

For the sauce, place the hot pan, used for the lamb, over a medium-high heat and pour in the wine, stirring to deglaze. Let bubble to reduce by half. Pour in the chicken stock, bring to the boil and simmer for 10 minutes.

Meanwhile, to finish the vegetables, heat a non-stick pan over a medium-high heat and add the knob of butter. Add the lemon skin and cook, stirring, for 1 minute without colouring. Add the chicken stock and bring to the boil. Add the broad beans and reheat for 2 minutes. Take off the heat and add the chopped lemon. Add the tomatoes just before serving and season with salt and pepper to taste.

Cover a plate with cling film, brush lightly with oil and lay the tarragon leaves for the garnish on top. Cover with another piece of cling film and microwave on high for 1–2 minutes till crisp. Meanwhile, reheat the potatoes in your oven for 2 minutes. Off the heat, whisk the butter into the sauce, a piece at a time, then add the chopped olives and tarragon. Pour into a warmed sauceboat.

To serve, cut the lamb racks in two and place on warmed plates. Arrange the vegetables on the plate with little spoonfuls of the black garlic purée. Finish with the crispy tarragon and serve with the sauce.

Crispy pork belly with taro

Serves 8

1.5kg pork belly
70g sea salt
4 pieces of pork fillet
  (tenderloin), about
  200g each
2 shallots, peeled and
  chopped
2 tbsp sugar
2 tbsp white wine vinegar
100ml brandy
400ml chicken stock
  (see page 184)
Olive oil for cooking
60g salted butter, in pieces
Sea salt and freshly ground
  black pepper

Crispy taro root (optional)

800g taro root, trimmed and
  peeled
2 tbsp olive oil

Creamed taro greens

Large bunch of taro leaves
  (20 medium leaves), or
  use spring greens
2 tbsp coconut oil or
  sunflower oil
1 onion, peeled and finely
  chopped
200ml chicken stock
  (see page 184)
400ml coconut cream

Using a very sharp knife, score the skin of the pork belly, first in one direction, then in the other, cutting across the first score lines. Place skin side up on a tray and rub the salt into the skin. Refrigerate for 2 hours.

Heat the oven to 230°C/Gas 8. Dust the salt off the pork and place, skin side up, in a roasting tray. Roast for 1 hour, then lower the oven setting to 130°C/Gas ½ and cook the pork for a further 1½ hours. Meanwhile, bring the pieces of pork fillet to room temperature, ready to cook.

While the pork is roasting, cut the taro root, if using, into batons, about 1.5cm thick and 6cm long, and toss in a bowl with the olive oil to coat well. When the pork is cooked, remove it to a warm platter; keep warm. Turn the setting up to 190°C/Gas 5. Bake the taro batons on an oven tray for about 25 minutes until cooked and crispy, turning occasionally.

Meanwhile, shred the taro (or spring green) leaves, discarding the central stem. Heat a medium casserole over a medium-high heat and drizzle in the coconut oil. Add the onion and cook for 1 minute. Add the taro leaves and sweat for 1 minute. Pour in the chicken stock and bring to the boil, then lower the heat to medium and cook for 5 minutes. Add the coconut cream and bring to the boil. Cook over a medium heat until most of the cream has been absorbed and the greens have reduced to a purée, about 10–15 minutes, seasoning with salt and pepper to taste.

Meanwhile, tip out the excess fat from the pork roasting tray, leaving about 1 tbsp. Add the shallots and stir over a medium-high heat for 1 minute. Add the sugar and cook, stirring, for a minute to caramelise, then add the wine vinegar. Pour in the brandy, stirring to deglaze, then add the chicken stock and bring to the boil. Pour into a saucepan and simmer over a medium heat to reduce for 10–15 minutes until thickened.

While the sauce is reducing, heat a non-stick frying pan and add a drizzle of olive oil. Add the pork fillet and colour well on all sides, then place in the oven to finish cooking for 7–10 minutes, turning halfway through cooking. Set aside to rest, with the pork belly. Whisk the butter into the sauce, a piece at a time, to finish.

To serve, cut the belly pork into pieces and slice the pieces of pork fillet in half. Spoon the creamed greens onto warm plates and arrange the pork belly and fillet on top, with the taro batons in the middle. Trickle the sauce over and around the pork; serve the rest in a jug.

In Samoa, pork is traditionally baked in hot rocks along with taro greens, which are filled with coconut cream then tied in banana leaf pouches.

Sticky rice with mangoes and Malibu ice cream

Serves 8

Sticky rice
100g black glutinous rice
100g red rice
400ml water
400ml coconut milk
60g palm sugar
100ml thin honey
Pinch of sea salt
2 cinnamon sticks
10 cardamom pods

Malibu ice cream
200ml milk
200ml coconut milk
100ml double cream
6 medium egg yolks
65g caster sugar
125ml Malibu

To serve
2 mangoes
Finely grated zest of
   1–2 limes
Dried lime slices to finish
   (see page 186), optional

Put the black and red rice into a bowl, pour on cold water to cover and leave to soak for 2 hours before cooking.

To make the ice cream, pour the milk, coconut milk and cream into a large heavy-based saucepan. Place over a medium-low heat and slowly bring to the boil. Meanwhile, whisk the egg yolks and caster sugar together in a large bowl. Pour about a third of the hot milk mixture onto the egg mixture, whisking as you do so, then pour this back into the pan, whisking again. Cook over a medium-low heat, stirring with a wooden spoon, until thickened enough to coat the back of the spoon. Remove from the heat.

Pass the custard through a sieve into a bowl and stir in the Malibu. Stand the bowl over another bowl of crushed ice to cool, stirring occasionally to prevent a skin forming, then churn in an ice-cream maker for about 20 minutes until firm.

Drain the black and red rice, place in a saucepan and pour on the 400ml water. Bring to the boil, then turn the heat down to medium and cook for about 25 minutes until just tender.

Meanwhile, put the coconut milk, palm sugar, honey, salt and spices into another saucepan and bring to the boil. Lower the heat and simmer for 5 minutes, then take off the heat and set aside.

Once the rice is cooked, strain the infused coconut milk onto it. Cook, stirring, over a medium heat for about 10 minutes until the consistency is thick and sticky. Remove from the heat and leave to stand for 5 minutes before serving; it will set slightly and turn dark brown.

Meanwhile, peel the mangoes and cut the flesh into long, fine ribbons with a mandoline or swivel vegetable peeler and arrange in nests on individual plates. Spoon the rice into the middle of the mango and top with a scoop of Malibu ice cream. Sprinkle with lime zest and stand a few dried lime slices on top to decorate if you like. Serve at once.

It's been a good few years since I first tried this wonderful sticky rice at my favourite Thai restaurant and I have added a little touch of my own to the dish.

Coconut buns *with rum*

Serves 6–7

100g plain white flour
200g strong white bread
  flour
Pinch of fine salt
10g fresh yeast
1 medium egg
50g sugar
55ml milk
55ml hot water (between
  hot and tepid)
Butter for greasing

Spice mix
20g soft brown sugar
1 tsp soft butter
Large pinch of ground
  cinnamon
Large pinch of freshly
  grated nutmeg

Coconut mix
500ml coconut milk
100g sugar
50g desiccated coconut
  or dried coconut flakes

To finish
150ml rum

In a large bowl, mix the flours and salt together. Crumble the yeast into another bowl, add the egg, sugar, milk and water and mix together well. Add this mixture to the dry ingredients and mix to a smooth dough. Continue to knead until the dough comes cleanly away from the bowl. (Use a mixer fitted with a dough hook if you have one.) Let the dough rest for 10 minutes, then knead again for 10 seconds. Repeat the resting and kneading once more, then leave to rest for another 10 minutes. Knead for a final 10 seconds, then cover and leave in a warm place to rest for 1 hour.

Butter 7 individual baking dishes or a 22cm square baking tray, 6cm deep (or tray with similar dimensions). For the spice mix, stir the ingredients together in a small bowl until evenly blended.

Split the dough in two, to make it easier to handle. Roll one portion out to a rectangle, about 30 x 20cm and spread half of the spice mix along the middle. Now fold the long sides over the spice mix and one another to enclose and form a roll (like a Swiss roll), moistening the edges with a little of the coconut milk to help seal them. Repeat with the other half.

Mix the coconut milk and sugar together and pour into the dishes or tray. Sprinkle liberally with the desiccated coconut or coconut shavings.

Slice the dough into short lengths: 2cm for individual dishes; 3cm if using a tray. Place side by side, cut side facing up, in the dishes or tray, leaving a 1cm gap in between if possible (it won't matter if one or two are closer).

Leave to prove in a warm place for about 40 minutes until doubled in size. Meanwhile, heat the oven to 190°C/Gas 5. Once the buns have risen, bake in the oven until golden brown; allow 8–10 minutes for individual dishes; 12–15 minutes for a tray. Let stand for 15 minutes before serving.

To serve, pour the rum into a small pan and bring to the boil, then set it alight. Immediately pour over the buns and serve, while still flaming.

I like to make these irresistible buns in individual dishes and flambé them with rum to serve, for an extra wow factor.

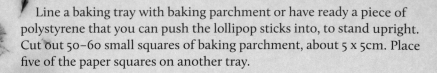

Makes 25–30

200g caster sugar
100g golden syrup
1 tsp baking powder
1 tsp lime juice
200g good-quality
   dark (or milk)
   chocolate,
   in pieces
25–30 small lolly
   sticks

Line a baking tray with baking parchment or have ready a piece of polystyrene that you can push the lollipop sticks into, to stand upright. Cut out 50–60 small squares of baking parchment, about 5 x 5cm. Place five of the paper squares on another tray.

Scatter the sugar in a wide heavy-based pan, add the golden syrup and place over a medium heat to melt. Cook to a golden caramel, stirring gently as it begins to colour; don't let it darken or it will taste bitter.

When the caramel is golden and bubbling, remove the pan from the heat and stir in the baking powder and lime juice; the mixture will bubble and foam dramatically.

Using a teaspoon, immediately put a spoonful of honeycomb onto each of the 5 paper squares and place a lolly stick in the middle. Place another square of parchment on top and press down gently.

Repeat to shape the rest of the honeycomb lollipops in batches of five, gently reheating the honeycomb in between as necessary (it will set as it cools). Once the honeycomb lollipops are firm, remove the paper squares.

Melt the chocolate in a heatproof bowl over a pan of barely simmering water, then remove from the heat, stir until smooth and let cool slightly. Dip the honeycomb lollipops into the melted chocolate and turn to coat. Either lay them on the lined tray or stand them in your polystyrene and leave to set.

These little lollipops are a great treat – especially for kids – and they are fun to make. I like to serve them with coffee at the end of a meal when I'm entertaining.

Basics

Pasta

Makes 4–6 servings

500g Italian 'oo' pasta flour
3 eggs
6 egg yolks
Pinch of salt

Put all the ingredients into a food processor or blender and blitz together to make a smooth dough that forms a ball. Wrap in cling film and leave to rest in the fridge for 30 minutes before using.

Divide the pasta into 4 portions and keep them well wrapped until ready to roll. Using a pasta machine, roll out each portion repeatedly, narrowing the setting by one notch each time, until you reach the desired thickness. Fit the appropriate cutters and cut the pasta as required into tagliatelle, pappardelle, spaghetti etc.

When ready to serve, add the pasta to a large saucepan of boiling salted water and cook for $1^{1}/_{2}$–2 minutes until al dente. Drain and serve.

NOTE You can prepare and cook the pasta ahead. After draining, refresh immediately in cold water and drain well. Store in a container drizzled with a little olive oil for up to 2 days. Simply add to a pan of boiling water and reheat briefly, then drain to serve.

Mayonnaise

Makes about 200ml

1 medium egg yolk,
  at room temperature
1 tsp Dijon mustard
1 tsp white wine vinegar
180ml rapeseed oil
sea salt and freshly ground
  pepper

Put the egg yolk, mustard and wine vinegar into a small bowl and whisk together until combined. Slowly add the oil in a thin trickle to begin with, whisking as you do so. As the mayonnaise begins to thicken, add the oil in a steady stream, still whisking all the time to emulsify.

When the oil is all incorporated, the mayonnaise should be thick and glossy. Season with salt and pepper to taste. Unless serving straight away, cover and refrigerate. It will keep for a couple of days in the fridge.

Chicken stock

Makes 1 litre

1kg chicken carcasses
  or wings
2 onions, peeled and
  quartered
3 celery sticks, cut into large
  chunks
1 leek (white part), washed
  and cut into chunks
2 litres water
Bouquet garni

Put the chicken bones or wings into a stockpot with the vegetables. Pour on the water to cover and bring to the boil. Skim off any scum from the surface, add the bouquet garni and turn down to a gentle simmer. Cook for 1 hour, skimming as necessary; do not allow to boil. Pass the stock through a conical sieve into a bowl and allow to cool. Refrigerate for up to 3–4 days until ready to use, or freeze in convenient batches.

BOUQUET GARNI I use a few thyme sprigs, a few parsley stalks, a bay leaf and the green part of the leek, tied together with kitchen string.

Brown chicken stock

Makes 1 litre

1.5kg chicken wings
2 tbsp olive oil
2 onions, peeled and
  roughly chopped
2 carrots, peeled and
  roughly chopped
4 celery sticks, roughly
  chopped
2 litres water

Heat the oven to 160°C/Gas 3. Lightly oil a large roasting tray and add the chicken wings, in a single layer. Roast in the oven for about 20 minutes until golden brown, turning once or twice to colour on all sides.

Place a large stockpot over a high heat and drizzle in the olive oil. Add the vegetables and colour for about 3–5 minutes until golden brown. Add the roasted chicken wings to the stockpot, then pour on the water to cover. Put the roasting tray over a medium heat and add a splash of water, stirring to deglaze, then tip the juices into the pot. Bring to the boil, skim off any scum from the surface and turn down to a gentle simmer. Cook for 1 hour, skimming as necessary; do not allow to boil. Pass the stock through a conical sieve into a bowl and allow to cool. Refrigerate for up to 3–4 days until ready to use, or freeze in convenient batches.

Vegetable stock

Makes 1 litre

2 onions, peeled
2 small carrots, peeled
1 small leek (white part),
  washed
2 celery sticks
1.5 litres water

Cut the vegetables into large chunks and place in a deep stockpot. Pour on the water to cover and bring to the boil. Lower the heat and simmer gently for about 45 minutes. Pass the stock through a conical sieve into a bowl and allow to cool. Refrigerate for up to 3–4 days until ready to use, or freeze in convenient batches.

NOTE I tend to add whatever vegetable trimmings I may have to hand to this basic recipe, such as ripe tomatoes or even just the skins, as well as herb stalks.

Veal stock

Makes about 700ml

1kg veal bones
1 calf's foot, split
  lengthways
Olive oil for drizzling
2 onions, peeled and
  roughly chopped
2 carrots, peeled and
  roughly chopped
4 celery sticks, roughly
  chopped
1 small leek (white part),
  washed and cut into
  chunks
2 tbsp tomato purée
2 litres water

Heat the oven to 190°C/Gas 5. Chop up the veal bones, place in a roasting tray with the calf's foot and drizzle with a little olive oil. Roast in the oven for 20 minutes or until well coloured. Add the vegetables to the roasting tray, stir and return to the oven for 5 minutes or so until the vegetables are golden brown.

Transfer the veal bones, calf's foot and vegetables to a large stockpot. Pour off any excess fat from the roasting tray and place over a medium heat. Add the tomato purée and cook, stirring, for 2 minutes, then add a splash of water to deglaze the tray. Tip this into the stockpot, then pour on the water to cover everything. Bring to the boil, skim off any scum from the surface and turn down to a gentle simmer. Cook for about 2 hours, skimming as necessary. Pass the stock through a conical sieve into a bowl and allow to cool. Refrigerate for up to 3–4 days until ready to use, or freeze in convenient batches.

Fish stock

Makes 1 litre

1kg white fish bones and
  trimmings (from sea bass,
  sole, turbot etc)
50ml olive oil
1 leek (white part), washed
  and cut into chunks
1 onion, peeled and roughly
  chopped
2 celery sticks, roughly
  chopped
3 garlic cloves, peeled and
  halved
150ml dry white wine
1.5 litres water
1 heaped tsp white
  peppercorns
Bouquet garni (see left)

Rinse the fish bones and trimmings and drain in a colander. Heat the olive oil in a stockpot and add the vegetables and garlic. Sweat over a medium heat for a few minutes, without colouring. Add the fish bones and cook gently for 2–3 minutes. Pour in the wine and let bubble to reduce by two-thirds. Now pour in the water to cover everything and add the peppercorns and bouquet garni. Bring to the boil, skim off any scum from the surface and turn down to a gentle simmer. Cook for about 20 minutes, skimming as necessary. Pass the stock through a conical sieve into a bowl and allow to cool. Refrigerate for up to 2 days until ready to use, or freeze in convenient batches.

Crème anglaise

Makes 500ml

400ml milk
100ml double cream
2 vanilla pods, halved
  lengthways
6 medium egg yolks
60g caster sugar
½ tsp natural vanilla extract

Pour the milk and cream into a heavy-based saucepan. Scrape out the seeds from the vanilla pods and add these to the pan along with the empty pods. Slowly bring to the boil. Meanwhile, whisk the egg yolks and sugar together in a bowl, then pour on the hot creamy milk, whisking as you do so. Return the mixture to the saucepan and cook, stirring, over a medium-low heat until the custard is thick enough to coat the back of the wooden spoon (at 82°C); do not allow to boil.

Immediately take off the heat and strain the crème anglaise through a fine-meshed sieve into a bowl. Stir in the vanilla extract. Chill over a bowl of iced water unless serving warm, straight away.

White chocolate crème anglaise

Chop 150g good-quality white chocolate into small pieces and place in a bowl. Prepare the crème anglaise as above, omitting the vanilla extract. As soon as it has thickened, remove from the heat and pour onto the chocolate, whisking as you do so. Continue until the chocolate has melted and the custard is smooth. Serve warm or cold.

Dried lime slices

1 lime
100ml water
80g caster sugar

Heat the oven to 160°C/Gas 3. Line a large baking sheet with non-stick baking parchment. Using a sharp knife, cut the lime into very thin slices, about 1.5mm, and place in a shallow dish. Put the water and sugar into a saucepan and dissolve over a medium heat. Bring to the boil, then remove from the heat and allow to cool. Pour the cooled sugar syrup over the lime slices and turn them to make sure they are well coated. Lay the lime slices on the lined baking sheet, cover with another sheet of parchment and lay a flat tray on top. Place in the oven for about 12 minutes to dry. Set aside to cool and dry, then store in an airtight container until ready to use.

Vanilla ice cream

Makes 1 litre

800ml whole milk
200ml double cream
4 vanilla pods, halved
  lengthways
12 medium egg yolks
125g caster sugar
1 tsp natural vanilla extract

Pour the milk and cream into a heavy-based saucepan. Scrape out the seeds from the vanilla pods and add these to the pan along with the empty pods. Slowly bring to the boil. Meanwhile, whisk the egg yolks and sugar together in a bowl, then pour on the hot creamy milk, whisking as you do so. Return the mixture to the saucepan and cook, stirring, over a medium-low heat until the custard is thick enough to coat the back of the wooden spoon (at 82°C); do not allow to boil.

Immediately remove from the heat and strain through a fine-meshed sieve into a bowl. Stir in the vanilla extract. Chill over a bowl of iced water, then transfer to an ice-cream maker and churn until set, about 15–20 minutes. Unless serving immediately, transfer to a freezerproof container and place in the freezer.

Ginger ice cream

Prepare the custard as for vanilla ice cream (above), omitting the vanilla extract, then whisk in 1 tbsp ground ginger while it is hot. Cool, chill and churn as above for about 15 minutes until thick but not set firm. Add 2 tbsp roughly chopped candied ginger and churn briefly to fold through. Serve or freeze as above.

Pistachio ice cream

Put 60g pistachio paste into a bowl. Prepare the custard as for vanilla ice cream (above), omitting the vanilla extract, then pour it onto the pistachio paste while it is hot, whisking as you do so. Cool, chill and churn as above for about 15 minutes until thick but not set firm. Add 2 tbsp roughly chopped (unsalted) pistachio nuts and churn briefly to fold through. Serve or freeze as above.

INDEX

Thank you to my family and dearest friends for loving me enough to let me go out into the world... Your love and faith in me has made all I have achieved possible.

Michel Roux Jr, thank you for opening the door to my culinary journey and the most amazing opportunities a chef could dream of. I couldn't have wished for a better mentor and friend.

Thanks to the amazing team on this book: Lucy, Janet, Yuki and Cynthia for making the vision become a reality. We worked hard but laughed through the majority of it.

Rachel Humphrey, I'm grateful to you for sourcing 'impossible' ingredients during winter photoshoots. Also to Beverly Downing, Renee Miller, Patricia Lefeuver and Toby Mosdale for all their help during the photoshoots. And to Francesco Dibenedetto who gobbled all the food while I tested the recipes.

And finally, my darling daughter Anais for reminding Mummy not to work too much and that it's important to stop for cuddles.